JOINT OPERATING AGREEMENTS: THE NEWSPAPER PRESERVATION ACT AND ITS APPLICATION

JOINT OPERATING AGREEMENTS: THE NEWSPAPER PRESERVATION ACT AND ITS APPLICATION

John C. Busterna

School of Journalism and Mass Communication
University of Minnesota

Robert G. Picard

Department of Communications
California State University, Fullerton

ABLEX PUBLISHING CORPORATION
NORWOOD, NEW JERSEY

Copyright © 1993 by Ablex Publishing Corporation

All rights reserved. No part of this publication may be reproduced, stored in a retrieval system, or transmitted, in any form or by any means, electronic, mechanical, photocopying, microfilming, recording or otherwise, without permission of the publisher.

Printed in the United States of America

Library of Congress Cataloging-in-Publication Data

Busterna, John C., 1952–
   Joint operating agreements : the Newspaper Preservation Act and its application / by John C. Busterna and Robert G. Picard.
     p.   cm.—(Communication and information science series)
   Includes bibliographical references and index.
   ISBN 0-89391-994-2 (cloth).—ISBN 1-56750-001-3 (pbk.)
   1. Press law—United States. 2. Antitrust law—United States.
3. Newspaper publishing—Government policy—United States.
I. Picard, Robert G. II. United States. Newspaper Preservation
Act. 1993 III. Title. IV. Series.
KF2750.B87 1993
343.73099'8—dc20
[347.303998]   93–11299
                                                                      CIP

Ablex Publishing Corporation
355 Chestnut Street
Norwood, New Jersey 07648

Table of Contents

List of Tables — vii

List of Figures — viii

Preface — ix

1 **The Nature of Newspaper Joint Operations** — *1*
   A Brief History of Joint Operations — *2*
   Definitions of Joint Operations — *4*
   Forms and Functions of JOAs — *6*
   Terms and Conditions of JOAs — *14*
   The Ebb and Flow of JOA Newspapers — *21*

2 **Development of Joint Operations and the Newspaper Preservation Act** — *25*
   Early Joint Operations — *26*
   The Citizen Publishing Case — *29*
   The Newspaper Preservation Act — *35*

3 **Application of the Newspaper Preservation Act** — *41*
   Applications Since Passage of the NPA — *43*
   Tests of Whether a Newspaper Is Failing — *51*
   Can Factors Causing Failure Be an Issue? — *57*

4	**Legislative Initiatives Regarding the NPA**	*63*
	S. 2314	*63*
	Amendment 2509 to S. 430	*68*
	House Judiciary Committee Oversight Hearings	*71*
	H. R. 4970	*72*
5	**Theory and Philosophy of the Newspaper Preservation Act**	*75*
	Some Economic Characteristics of the Newspaper Industry	*76*
	Economic Performance Criteria	*83*
	JOAs and Content Performance	*88*
6	**Empirical Studies of JOA Newspaper Performance**	*93*
	Empirical Studies of Economic Performance	*94*
	Empirical Studies of Content Performance	*99*
	Summary of Findings	*109*
7	**Failures of the Newspaper Preservation Act**	*111*
	Failed and Dissolved JOAs	*113*
	The Potential for Future Failures	*118*
8	**Implications for Public Policy**	*121*
	A Policy to Preserve Newspapers	*122*
	A Policy to Promote Editorial Competition	*125*
	A Policy to Minimize the Loss of Economic Competition	*126*
	A Policy to Maximize Cost Savings to Consumers	*128*
	Implementing Limited Joint Operations	*130*
	Summary	*133*
	Exhibit 1: Amended Newspaper Preservation Act	*135*
Appendix A: Text of the Newspaper Preservation Act		*138*
Appendix B: Tucson Modified Joint Operating Agreement		*141*
References and Bibliography		*147*
Author Index		*163*
Subject Index		*167*

List of Tables

1.1	Newspapers in Joint Operations By Ownership and Beginning and Expiration Dates	*8*
1.2	JOAs By Joint Venture/Operating Partner Structures	*12*
1.3	Joint Operating Newspapers By Ownership	*13*
1.4	Duration of Joint Operations	*15*
1.5	Revenue Division in JOAs	*17*
1.6	Formulae For Covering Losses	*18*
1.7	Composition Of Joint Operation Management and Requirements For Decisions	*20*
1.8	JOAs Sought Since Passage Of the Newspaper Preservation Act	*22*
1.9	Joint Operations That Have Ceased Publication Or Ended	*23*
2.1	Trends in Competitive Daily Newspaper Cities, 1880–1986	*26*
3.1	Indicators of Failure in Newspapers Seeking JOA Approvals	*58*
3.2	Recommendations on Applications by the Antitrust Division	*60*
3.3	Actions by the Attorney General on Approval and Nonapproval Recommendations	*61*
5.1	Forms of Newspaper Competition and Economic Performance	*88*

List of Figures

1.1	Structure of Joint Venture Operating Companies	*10*
1.2	Structure of Operating Partner Joint Operating Agreements	*11*
3.1	Process for Gaining JOA Approval	*43*
3.2	Disparity Between Advertising and Circulation Shares in Newspapers Entering JOAs Since 1970	*54*
4.1	S. 2314 as Introduced	*64*
4.2	S. 2314 as Reported From Committee	*67*
4.3	Senate Amendment 2509 to S. 430	*69*
4.4	H. R. 4970	*73*
5.1	A Welfare Economics Model of Efficiency and Equity in Newspaper Markets	*85*

Preface

This is a book about public policy gone awry in the newspaper industry. The Newspaper Preservation Act (NPA) of 1970 was enacted with the stated goals of preserving trailing newspapers in two-newspaper markets. The NPA acknowledged that it permitted the cessation of advertising and circulation competition between the newspapers, but allowed editorial competition to continue. This special interest legislation was both unnecessary to preserve trailing newspapers and harmful to its purported goals.

This book shows that the NPA has not succeeded in preserving these trailing newspapers, but rather has hastened their decline. The NPA succeeds in ending advertising and circulation competition, and it also creates a disincentive for newspapers to compete with each other editorially. Furthermore, the book demonstrates that the cost-sharing arrangements purported to be made by the NPA can exist, virtually in their entirety, without the NPA.

Chapter 1 presents detailed information about current joint operating agreements (JOAs) among formerly competitive newspapers throughout the United States. The second chapter analyzes the *Citizen Publishing* case which outlawed 7-day-a-week price fixing and profit pooling, and describes Congressional actions which provided newspapers with an antitrust exemption to permit them to circumvent the Supreme Court decision. Chapter 3 discusses how the NPA has been applied to newspapers forming new JOAs since the passage of the NPA. The fourth chapter details the unsuccessful attempts to amend or repeal the NPA.

Chapter 5 presents the theoretical economic and content performance goals that public policy should achieve, while the sixth chapter provides an analysis of the relevant empirical studies. The seventh chapter discusses those instances in which exiting JOAs have been discontinued, and presents a list of other joint operations in which failure may soon come.

Chapter 8 summarizes the case this book has made: Modified joint operations, such as the one permitted in Tucson before the passage of the NPA, provide a superior policy option to the current NPA. These modified joint operations would provide the same cost-saving operations of JOAs under the NPA, including a jointly produced Sunday paper and a combination advertising rate for the other six days of the week, but require the newspapers to compete for advertising and circulation on those days. The type of joint operation proposed here has the significant added advantage of not requiring one of the partners to be a failing newspaper. Thus, any currently competing newspapers can form joint operations without waiting until one newspaper is on its death bed when a joint operation will appear less appealing to the stronger newspaper.

These modified operations can be accomplished either by amending the NPA or by abolishing it and allowing newspapers to enter court-approved consent decrees as in the Tucson case. The policy option suggested here is revolutionary, because it was not considered by Congress when it adopted the NPA, nor by either the NPA's proponents or opponents during deliberations on the act or since its passage. The previous policy discussion has been limited to the belief that fully separated competitive newspapers are the only alternative to the 7-day-a-week cartels permitted by the NPA.

The book should be useful for students and scholars of newspaper economics, management, and public policy for its extensive descriptive treatment of JOAs, review of theory and the research literature, and for the new policy option it brings to the debate. The book may have its greatest practical value by informing the managements of the relatively few remaining competing newspapers that another alternative is available to them that will permit far more profitable operations than their current competitive situation, yet avoid the failing newspaper requirement and legal rigmarole of the NPA. Perhaps some of these competitive newspapers can be preserved by adopting the modified joint operations proposed here and by ignoring the NPA altogether.

Newspapers operating under the current NPA continue to have their problems. Since the book manuscript went to press, the JOA in Pittsburgh has dissolved with the owners of the *Post-Gazette* purchasing the *Press* and then shutting it down January 18, 1993. Also in January, the JOA in Honolulu experienced a shake-up. Gannett sold its afternoon 88,000 circulation *Star-Bulletin* to Liberty Newspapers after purchasing the stronger morning *Honolulu Advertiser* with 105,000 circulation from its former JOA partner Persis Corp. The newly formed JOA has an agreement to continue for another 20 years. During the same month in the previously competitive San Antonio market, the *Light* ceased publication, giving monopoly control to the surviving *Express-News* without choosing the JOA option available under the NPA. Perhaps if other competitive newspapers were made aware of the modified joint operation option presented here, some of these newspapers will not go the way of the San Antonio *Light*.

The authors would like to acknowledge the assistance of Emil Rould of Tucson Newspapers, Inc., who discussed the modified agreement that existed in Tucson before the passage of the NPA, and who provided the text of that consent decree which is presented in Appendix B of this book. We also appreciate the thorough preliminary editing of the manuscript by Elizabeth Carpelan before the final version of the manuscript was delivered into the very capable hands of production coordinator Teresa Faella and others at Ablex.

1
The Nature of Newspaper Joint Operations

Joint operations are created when two or more newspapers agree to combine some operations as a means of cost sharing and reducing operating costs. These formalized agreements of cooperation are mutually beneficial to newspapers because they reduce the relatively high costs associated with the production and distribution aspects of the newspaper industry and the difficulty of maintaining more than one daily newspaper in a market.

If joint operations did no more than share costs, such arrangements would generate little controversy. However, nearly all joint operating newspapers engage in a variety of actions that are anticompetitive restraints of trade. These acts (price fixing, profit pooling, and market allocation) have generated significant criticism and government antitrust litigation.

When their operations were found to violate antitrust laws in the late 1960s, existing joint operating newspapers sought and received from Congress a special antitrust exemption called the Newspaper Preservation Act (NPA) that permitted them to engage in these normally prohibited activities. The act also provided a mechanism for other newspapers to apply for the exemption. The law passed without the controversy it might have generated had another industry been involved. The lack of controversy was partially due to the lack of media coverage given to the proposed measures and Congressional hearings on the NPA.

In this book, we will use the term *joint operating agreement* or *JOA* only when we refer to an agreement or activity that specifically exists under, or is permitted by, the Newspaper Preservation Act. The term *joint operation* will be used as a more general reference or to an agreement or activity that exists outside the scope of the NPA or occurred before the act's passage.

Since the passage of the NPA, publishers of JOA newspapers have unsuccessfully sought to obtain legislative approval to expand the scope of activities of JOA firms. Opponents have begun serious efforts to recind or revise the NPA. Much of that action has generated little press coverage as well.

However, recent activities have garnered some coverage in the trade press and have led many industry observers and policy makers to pay closer attention to the NPA and its effects. These activities include the controversies over the approval of a JOA between the Detroit newspapers and payments to Cox Newspapers to close its JOA newspaper in Miami. In addition, disputes have arisen over the exercise of market power by JOA newspapers nationwide. Finally, there have been growing discussions over the role of apparently deliberate efforts by management to cause their newspapers to fail in order to qualify for the antitrust exemption granted by the NPA (see, for example, Busterna, 1987b, 1988c; Peterson, 1990; Picard, 1988b; Steel, 1989).

A BRIEF HISTORY OF JOINT OPERATIONS

Many casual newspaper observers believe that the development of joint operating agreements among newspapers is a relatively new phenomenon, but the history of such arrangements is at least six decades old.

The first known joint newspaper operation began in 1933 when the *Albuquerque* (NM) *Journal* and *The Albuquerque Tribune* joined all but their editorial operations—an arrangement that continues to this day—and established a model that many joint operations would follow.

In the 1930s, newspapers in three other cities created operating combinations: El Paso, TX, in 1936; Nashville, TN, in 1937; and Evansville, IN, in 1938.

Four cities became the sites of joint arrangements in the 1940s: Tucson, AZ, in 1940; Tulsa, OK, in 1941; Chattanooga, TN, in 1942; and Madison, WI, in 1948.

Sixteen papers in eight cities combined in the 1950s: Birmingham, AL, Fort Wayne, ID, and Lincoln, NE, in 1950; Salt Lake City, UT, in 1952; Shreveport, LA, in 1953; Knoxville, TN, in 1957; Charleston, WV, in 1958; and St. Louis, MO, in 1959.

In the 1960s, four more papers established joint operations: Pittsburgh, PA, in 1961; Honolulu, HI, in 1962; San Francisco, CA, in 1965; and Miami, FL, in 1966.

In 1965, the U.S. Department of Justice challenged an agreement to renew the joint operation of the Tucson newspapers on antitrust grounds, a challenge that was upheld by the U.S. Supreme Court in 1969.

As that case worked its way through the federal court system, publishers of other newspapers with combined operations—realizing their legal vulnerability—gained the support of the American Newspaper Publishers Association and began lobbying Congress to exempt existing joint operations from antitrust laws. They argued that the exemption was necessary to save newspapers from dying across the country. In 1970, Congress passed the Newspaper Preservation Act, exempting previous joint operations from antitrust laws and providing a mechanism for potential new joint operations to apply for approval.

After passage of the act, two cities became the sites of JOAs in the 1970s: Anchorage, AK, in 1974 and Cincinnati, OH, in 1979.

During the 1980s, newspapers in three cities established combined operations: Chattanooga, TN, in 1980; Seattle, WA, in 1982; and Detroit, MI, in 1988.

So far in the 1990s, JOAs have been established in Las Vegas, NV, and York, PA, both in 1990.

During the 1980s, opposition to JOAs began to mount among newspaper publishers who argued that JOA newspapers were using their antitrust exemptions to compete unfairly with suburban and nondaily newspapers. When litigation raised significant questions about the scope of the antitrust exemptions, publishers of JOA newspapers asked Congress to specifically widen the exemption. Those efforts generated significant opposition from non-JOA publishers, who blocked the bills that would have expanded the exemption.

The opposition grew so strong that in 1990 and 1991, JOA opponents had bills introduced in Congress to repeal the Newspaper Preservation Act altogether, but those bills never reached committee.

Since the development of the idea of the Newspaper Preservation Act in the 1960s, many proponents of JOAs have argued that JOAs were established in response to suburbanization and the decay of large metropolitan cities and that the act is intended to overcome those problems. That argument, however, is not borne out by the history of joint operations.

The legislative history of the act is clearly linked to the antitrust action against the Tucson newspapers, and the establishment dates and locations of most JOA newspapers run counter to the assertion that JOAs were established to save large metropolitan newspapers harmed by suburbanization.

If one looks at the pattern of establishment of joint operations, one finds that 20 agreements were established between 1930 and 1970, prior to the existence of the NPA. Eight were established well before the significant development of metropolitan suburbs.

A review of location shows that most joint operating newspapers were established in, and continue to operate in, communities that were not large metropolitan areas. Of joint operations established in 18 cities after 1950—when suburbanization could have become a factor—only five locations ranked in the top 20 metropolitan areas: Pittsburgh, San Francisco, and Detroit in the top 10, and Miami and St. Louis in the top 20. The majority of JOA newspapers were established and operate in small- and mid-sized markets.

Two main factors make it difficult for more than one newspaper to publish in a market. First, economies of scale benefit larger newspapers. Second, many advertisers place advertisements in only the larger circulation newspaper. These two factors are crucial to understanding newspaper costs, newspaper mortality, and the incentives and disincentives for creating joint operating agreements. They will be discussed further in Chapter 5.

DEFINITIONS OF JOINT OPERATIONS

Although these joint operating agreements are usually made between competing newspapers published in the same geographic markets, in broader terms they can also be created between newspapers in different geographical markets to establish a centralized facility to handle operations. This occurred, for example, when Thomson Corporation and Media News Group created a joint venture to publish the Pasadena *Star-News*, *San Gabriel Valley Daily Tribune*, Whittier *Daily News*, and four weeklies in 1989. Although their agreement created a joint operation, it did not involve the antitrust concerns that most associate with the term *joint operating agreement*.

Joint operating agreements between newspapers should not be confused with joint newspaper monopolies, a term used when a single company owns two newspapers in a market, such as Cox Enterprises which publishes the morning *Constitution* and evening *Journal* in Atlanta, GA. Although the financial and economic benefits of joint operations are similar, the two structures are distinguishable by the separate ownership evident in JOAs.

Another cooperative form of publishing occurs when publishers of weekly newspapers contract for services from other weekly and daily newspapers. Some casual observers may confuse these to be forms of joint operations similar to JOAs that operate under the Newspaper

Preservation Act. However, they usually involve only production and printing contracts; thus these agreements do not have any anticompetitive components, such as price fixing and profit pooling.

Joint operations do not represent mergers of the firms involved. In a joint operation, the companies remain separate but enter the agreements when they either contract for services from each other or form a separate, joint-owned firm to carry out common operations. In order to create a joint operation, both partners must be willing to enter the agreement and negotiate terms that are acceptable to both firms. If one firm refuses to enter the joint operation or rejects its terms, no agreement can be created.

Joint operations can be created that do not involve any activities that would normally violate the antitrust laws without the NPA exemption. These joint operations involve newspapers that combine their advertising and circulation operations, share production and printing facilities, and merge administrative operations, including accounting, personnel, and promotion departments. Such efforts make it possible for the newspapers to centralize operations in one location, thus eliminating the need for duplicative facilities, equipment, and functions. This makes it possible to operate with fewer employees than if the newspapers operated separately. In addition to the cost savings and economies of scale resulting from these joint operations, joint operating newspapers can obtain pecuniary economies through bulk discount purchases of larger quantities of supplies.

There is a common misconception that these types of joint operations are illegal and would not be permissible without the NPA. This misconception has been promoted by JOA publishers since they began lobbying for the NPA in the 1960s. Their rhetoric has misled many observers and officials to accept the view that the NPA is necessary to save from failure those newspapers currently in JOAs and some of the few remaining competing newspapers that may enter JOAs in the future (see, for example, Lacy, 1990a; Lewenstein & Rosse, 1988).

However, this view is erroneous because many joint operation and cost sharing activities are not prohibited by antitrust laws, even without the protection of the exemption provided by the NPA. Joint operations only conflict with antitrust laws when they also involve price fixing, market allocation, and profit pooling (see Goldsmith, 1977; Newspaper Guild v. Levi, 1976). Later in the book it will be argued that even without the NPA, price fixing and profit pooling appears to be permitted between newspapers for a jointly produced Sunday edition.

In 1965, the U.S. Department of Justice challenged the joint operation between the *Tucson Citizen* and *The Arizona Daily Star*. A federal district court and the U.S. Supreme Court found the price fixing, profit pooling, and market allocation aspects to violate the Sherman Antitrust Act, but found the cost sharing aspects of the agreement permissible.

After intense lobbying by some newspaper companies and associations, Congress passed the NPA exemption for the illegal activities. Congress justified the NPA as a means of slowing newspaper mortality and preserving editorial competition. The NPA specified criteria needed to qualify for the exemption, and provided an application mechanism for approval of new JOAs.

Many commentators in the trade and academic literature have argued that Congress' rhetoric notwithstanding, the real intent of the legislation was to protect the cartel profits of the few newspaper companies that had portions of their joint operations placed in jeopardy by the Tucson litigation.

Since its passage, the NPA has been more effective in preserving JOA newspapers than in preventing the deaths of competitive newspapers, but even that success has been limited. For example, between 1978 and 1982, more than 30 competing newspapers chose monopoly while only three chose to apply for JOAs (Radolf, 1982).

One limitation on the NPA's ability to save newspapers is that its intervention would occur on the deathbed of many failing newspapers, when there is little incentive for the leading newspaper to join a JOA but great incentive to wait for the other newspaper's death and gain a monopoly (Patkus, 1984).

Preexisting joint newspaper operations that were "grandparented" under the NPA have not been fully maintained. Preexisting JOA newspapers in Columbus, Knoxville, Miami, St. Louis, Tulsa, and Shreveport have ceased publishing, and observers expect several other JOA newspapers to do so in the next decade.

Today, 36 daily newspapers in 18 cities operate under the provisions of the NPA and four daily newspapers in two other cities have joint operations that are not covered by the NPA (Table 1.1).

This chapter has mentioned several means by which joint operations may exist, but this book will focus on the more narrowly structured JOAs, agreements that are customarily made between daily newspapers operating in the same market that are governed by the NPA. However, because of their history and related structure the book also includes discussion of the two joint operations in Lincoln, NE, and Madison, WI, that are not covered by the NPA.

FORMS AND FUNCTIONS OF JOAs

Information about the structures, operations, and terms of individual joint operations is difficult to acquire. When asked for copies of their

Table 1.1. Newspapers in Joint Operations By Ownership and Beginning and Expiration Dates

City/Newspapers	Ownership	Agreement Dates	Year Expires
Joint Operations Under the Newspaper Preservation Act			
Albuquerque, NM		1933	2022
Journal	Independent	1939 amend	
Tribune	Scripps-Howard	1953 amend	
		1957 amend	
		1960 amend	
		1967 amend	
		1972 amend	
		1979 amend	
		1982 amend	
		1982 amend	
Birmingham, AL		1950	2015
Post-Herald	Scripps-Howard	1956 amend	
News	Newhouse	1978 amend	
		1988 amend	
Charleston, WV		1958	2036
Gazette	Independent	1967 amend	
Daily Mail	Thomson	1970 suppl.	
		1973 amend	
		1986 amend	
Chattanooga, TN		1942	
Times	Independent	1966 dissolved	
News-Free Press	Independent	1980 reestab.	2000
Cincinnati, OH		1977	2007
Enquirer	Gannett		
Post	Scripps-Howard		
Detroit, MI		1989	2086
Free Press	Knight-Ridder		
News	Gannett		
El Paso, TX		1936	2015
Times	Gannett	1981 amend	
Herald-Post	Scripps-Howard	1985 renew & amend	
		1989 amend	
Evansville, IN		1938	1998
Courier	Independent	1986 amend	
Press	Scripps-Howard		
Fort Wayne, IN		1950	2020
Journal-Gazette	Independent	1954 amend	
News-Sentinel	Knight-Ridder	1957 amend	
		1974 amend	
		1980 amend	

Table 1.1. Newspapers in Joint Operations By Ownership and Beginning and Expiration Dates *(cont'd.)*

City / Papers	Ownership	Begin / Amendments	End
Honolulu, HI		1962	2042
Advertiser	Independent	1962 amend	
Star-Bulletin	Gannett	1963 amend	
		1964 amend	
		1965 amend	
		1966 amend	
		1981 amend	
Las Vegas, NV		1989	2049
Review Journal	Donrey		
Sun	Independent		
Nashville, TN		1937	2022
Tennessean	Gannett	1967 amend	
Banner	Independent	1979 amend	
		1986 amend	
Pittsburgh, PA		1961	1999
Post-Gazette	Block		
Press	Scripps-Howard		
Salt Lake City, UT		1952	2012
Tribune	Independent	1982 renew &	
Deseret News	Independent	amend	
San Francisco, CA		1965	1995
Chronicle	Chronicle Publ.		
Examiner	Hearst		
Seattle, WA		1983	2032
Post-Intelligencer	Hearst		
Times	Seattle Times	(49.5% Knight-Ridder)	
Tucson, AZ		1940	2015
Star	Pulitzer	1953 amend	
Citizen	Gannett	1965 renew	
		1970 amend	
		1988 renew	
York, PA		1989	2090
Record	Buckner		
Dispatch	Media News		

Joint Operations Not Covered by the NPA

City / Papers	Ownership	Year	
Lincoln, NE		1950	
Star	Lee		
Journal	Independent		
Madison, WI		1948	
Wis. State Journal	Lee		
Capital Times	Independent		

THE NATURE OF NEWSPAPER JOINT OPERATIONS 9

Table 1.1. Newspapers in Joint Operations By Ownership and Beginning and Expiration Dates (*cont'd.*)

Joint Operations in Effect But Not Publishing

Miami, FL		1966	2021
Herald	Knight-Ridder	1971 amend	
News (ceased)	Cox	1987 amend	
St. Louis, MO		1959	2014
Post-Dispatch	Pulitzer	1961 amend	
Globe-Democrat	Newhouse	1975 renegotiate	
(ceased)		1979 amend	
		1983 amend	

JOA Applications Withdrawn

Manteca, CA		1988
Bulletin	Morris	
News	Independent	

agreements, most publishers refuse to make them available, saying they contain proprietary business information. Some information is available in court documents when JOA-related activities have been the subject of litigation. Some is available in the public files of the U.S. Department of Justice. Post-NPA applicants provided extensive information to the Justice Department and those altering preexisting agreements have been required to file the changes with the Justice Department as well.

Publishers' desires to keep information from the public despite their request for special treatment under the antitrust laws has existed for most of the history of the NPA. Since its passage, publishers have unsuccessfully opposed even publishing notices in their newspapers that they were seeking approval of a JOA, and sought to halt public disclosure of all business and financial data (Huston, 1972; Keep, 1982). In gathering the information for this section, public files at the Department of Justice, court records, materials provided to legislative hearings, and information provided by publishers to the authors have been used as sources.

Arrangements for combining operations take two major forms: (a) joint ventures, and (b) operating partnerships.

Joint ventures are formed when the participating newspapers form a separate company to provide the joint services to the newspapers (Figure 1.1). In most cases, the new firm is jointly owned by both newspaper companies.

The joint firm is capitalized by the two newspapers contributing

10 JOINT OPERATING AGREEMENTS

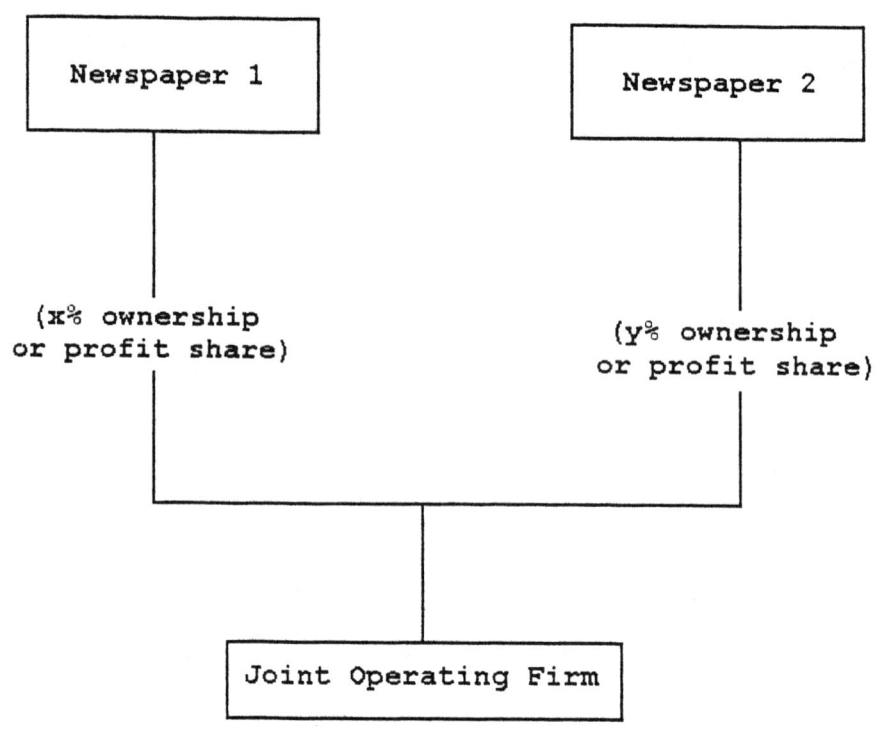

```
┌─────────────────┐              ┌─────────────────┐
│  Newspaper 1    │              │  Newspaper 2    │
└────────┬────────┘              └────────┬────────┘
         │                                │
  (x% ownership                    (y% ownership
   or profit share)                 or profit share)
         │                                │
         └───────────────┬────────────────┘
                        │
                ┌───────┴──────────┐
                │ Joint Operating Firm │
                └──────────────────────┘
```

Figure 1.1. Structure Of Joint Venture Operating Companies

land, buildings, equipment, supplies, and cash. The new firm is managed by a board of directors made up of executives from, or individuals selected by, the two newspaper firms. When contributions of the two firms are equal, they typically split ownership and profits of the joint firm on a 50–50 basis. If contributions are unequal, ownership and profits are split favoring the firm that provides the largest amount of capital.

In this type of arrangement, the two firms continue to exist and separately produce the editorial content of each newspaper. The joint venture firm is normally responsible for the other aspects of production, distribution, advertising sales, marketing, and so on.

The second type of JOA structure is the one in which one newspaper acts as the operating partner for the other, providing printing and other services under contract (Figure 1.2). No third joint venture firm is created under this arrangement, but this JOA type operates along similar lines of the joint venture JOAs by combining many operations in one firm that serves as the operating partner. Sometimes these arrangements include an initial contribution of facilities, equipment, cash, etc., from the secondary partner to the firm providing services.

THE NATURE OF NEWSPAPER JOINT OPERATIONS   11

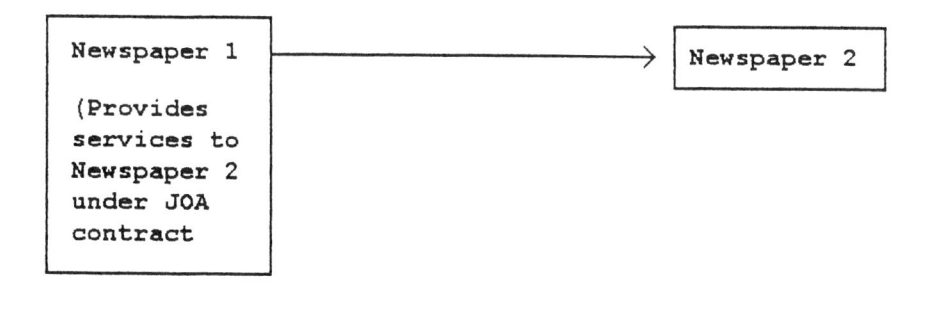

```
┌─────────────┐                          ┌─────────────┐
│ Newspaper 1 │─────────────────────────▶│ Newspaper 2 │
│             │                          └─────────────┘
│ (Provides   │
│ services to │
│ Newspaper 2 │
│ under JOA   │
│ contract    │
└─────────────┘
```

or, alternately,

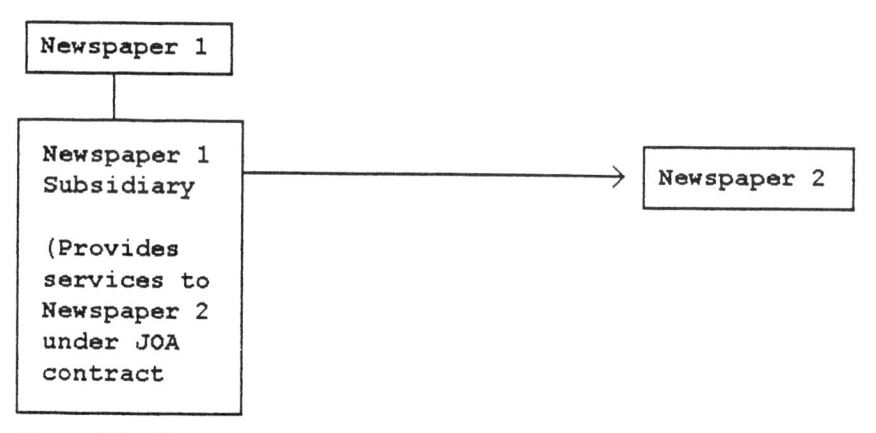

```
┌─────────────┐
│ Newspaper 1 │
└──────┬──────┘
       │
┌─────────────┐                          ┌─────────────┐
│ Newspaper 1 │─────────────────────────▶│ Newspaper 2 │
│ Subsidiary  │                          └─────────────┘
│             │
│ (Provides   │
│ services to │
│ Newspaper 2 │
│ under JOA   │
│ contract    │
└─────────────┘
```

Figure 1.2. Structure Of Operating Partner Joint Operating Agreements

Services to the joint operations can be provided either directly by the managing newspaper or through a subsidiary it creates to handle the joint activities.

Joint venture and operating partnership arrangements are found equally among operations covered by the NPA. Nine out of the 18 current JOAs use the joint venture, separate company structure (Table 1.2). The two non-NPA joint operations in Madison, WI, and Lincoln, NE, are both joint venture arrangements.

In recent years, some preexisting JOAs have begun moving away from joint venture arrangements toward operating partnership structures when contract renewals have been made. This occurred, for example, when JOA contracts were renewed in El Paso and Nashville.

Among companies that own multiple JOA newspapers, no pattern of preferred structure emerges. Gannett, Scripps-Howard, Knight-Rid-

Table 1.2. JOAs By Joint Venture/Operating Partner Structures

City	Joint Venture Firm	Operating Partner
Newspapers Covered by the NPA		
Albuquerque	Albuquerque Publishing Co.	
Birmingham		*News*
Charleston	Newspaper Agency Corp.	
Chattanooga		*News-Free Press*
Cincinnati		*Enquirer*
Detroit	Detroit Newspaper Agency	
El Paso		*Times*
Evansville		*Press*
Fort Wayne	Agency Corp.	
Honolulu	Hawaii Newspaper Agency	
Las Vegas		*Review-Journal*
Nashville		*Tennessean*
Pittsburgh		*Press*
Salt Lake	Newspaper Agency Corp.	
San Francisco	San Fran. Newspaper Agency	
Seattle		*Times*
Tucson	Tucson Newspapers, Inc.	
York	York Newspaper Company	
Non-NPA Joint Operations		
Madison	Madison Newspapers, Inc.	
Lincoln	Journal-Star Printing Co.	
Joint Agreements in Effect		
Miami		*Herald*
St. Louis		*Post-Dispatch*
JOA Applications Withdrawn		
Manteca	Manteca Newspaper Agency	
JOAs Ceased Operating		
Anchorage		*Times*
Columbus		*Dispatch*
Knoxville		*News Sentinel*
Oil City-Franklin	Venango Newspapers	

Shreveport	Newspaper Production Co.
Tulsa	Newspaper Printing Corp.

der, and Hearst each have newspapers split between joint venture and operating partnership structures, although Gannett appears to be moving to take greater control of its markets by shifting to operating partnerships whenever possible.

Ownership of JOA Newspapers

Under the NPA, ownership of newspapers in JOAs is not at issue and newspapers may be either independently or group owned. This factor became more important after *The Cincinnati Enquirer* and *The Cincinnati Post* JOA hearings in 1979. An administrative law judge ruled that the financial condition of a failing newspaper's parent corporation should not be a factor in deciding whether or not to grant approval.

The judge's interpretation was especially important for newspaper chains because only about one-third of JOA newspapers are not owned by chains. Gannett and Scripps-Howard each own 6 JOA newspapers (Table 1.3).

Table 1.3. Joint Operating Newspapers By Ownership

Group	Number	Percent
Newspaper Preservation Act Newspapers		
Block Newspapers	1	2.8
Buckner News Alliance	1	2.8
Chronicle Publishing	1	2.8
Donrey	1	2.8
Gannett	6	16.7
Garden State (Media News)	1	2.8
Hearst	2	5.6
Independent	13	30.6
Knight-Ridder	2*	5.6
Newhouse	1	2.8
Pulitzer	1	2.8
Scripps-Howard	6	16.7
Seattle Times Co.	1*	2.8
Thomson	1	2.8
Joint Operating Newspapers Not Covered by NPA		
Independent	2	50.0
Lee Enterprises	2	50.0

*Excluding 49.5% ownership of Seattle Times Company by Knight-Ridder.

The protections afforded chain owners and their purchases of JOA newspapers after the NPA was passed has led some critics to charge that the NPA favors chain ownership and has been effective in reducing rather than "increasing the number of separate newspaper owners" (Barnett, 1980a, p. 41).

TERMS AND CONDITIONS OF JOAs

The terms and conditions of JOAs are negotiated between participating newspapers during the creation of JOAs (or they were grand-parented in for JOAs that existed before passage of the NPA). These terms involve issues of the duration of the agreement, revenue or profit division, contingencies for losses, management of joint firms and contracts, and so on.

Duration and Renewal

The length of time the agreement will be in force varies widely, ranging from 20 to 100 years among the existing JOAs. Although earlier agreements provided shorter time periods, more recent agreements have tended to increase the time period. In addition to the initial contract period, many agreements provide for renewals and extensions of the contract. Some renewals are automatic; others provide the option but require specific action. In most cases, a newspaper that wishes to end the JOA or renegotiate the terms of the agreement at the end of the contract period must provide at least two years' warning that it does not intend to renew the contract at the end of its term. The length of contracts for existing and ceased JOAs are shown in Table 1.4.

Revenue Division

Revenue from the joint firm is divided between the newspaper owners based on a predetermined percentage of revenue or on their percentage of ownership of the new firm. In rare cases, profits are divided based on performance measures in circulation and/or advertising sales.

In most cases a special division of the profits is made in the first years of operation to adjust for differing capital contributions of the partners to their joint ventures or to provide payments for exchange or acquisition of equipment or real estate needed by the operating partnership newspaper when no joint venture is created. In some cases, contracts provide revenue division or payments on sliding scales

Table 1.4. Duration Of Joint Operations

City	Duration of Existing Contract	Renewal Periods/Terms
Currently Existing Agreements		
Albuquerque	40 years	1 year/automatic unless 3-year nonrenewal notice is given
Birmingham	27 years	10 years/requires 2-year renewal request/1-year nonrenewal notice
Charleston	50 years	None/to be negotiated
Chattanooga	20 years	None/to be negotiated; 5-year nonrenewal notice for *News-Free Press*; 3-year nonrenewal notice for *Times*
Cincinnati	30 years	10 years/automatic unless nonrenewal notice is given
Detroit	100 years	25 years/automatic unless nonrenewal notice is given
El Paso	30 years	10 years/automatic unless nonrenewal notice is given
Evansville	12 years	10 years/automatic unless 15-year nonrenewal notice is given
Fort Wayne	unavailable lasts until 2020	2-year nonrenewal notice is required
Honolulu	unavailable lasts until 2042	unavailable
Las Vegas	50 years	10 years/automatic unless nonrenewal notice is given
Miami	33 years	not renewable
Nashville	35 years	2 years/automatic unless 2-year nonrenewal notice is given
Pittsburgh	unavailable lasts until 1999	unavailable
Salt Lake City	30 years	5 years/automatic unless 2-year nonrenewal notice is given; *News* has a 10-year renewal option with 2-year notice
San Francisco	30 years	10 years/required if either party requests renewal
Seattle	50 years	10 years/automatic unless nonrenewal notice is given
St. Louis	35 years	in effect; 3 30-year renewal options; 5-year nonrenewal notice is required

16   JOINT OPERATING AGREEMENTS

Tucson	25 years	25 years/automatic unless nonrenewal notice is given
York	100 years	25 years/automatic unless 5-year nonrenewal notice is given
Joint Operations Not Covered by NPA		
Lincoln	unavailable	unavailable
Madison	5 years	5 years/automatic unless nonrenewal notice is given
JOAs Ended		
Anchorage	30 years	2 years/nonrenewal notice is required
Columbus	25 years	2 years/nonrenewal notice is required
Knoxville	20 years	10 years/automatic unless 2-year nonrenewal notice is given
Oil City-Franklin	unavailable	unavailable
Shreveport	35 years	13 years/automatic unless 2-year nonrenewal notice is given
Tulsa	15 years	1 year/automatic unless 3-year nonrenewal notice is given
JOA Applications Withdrawn		
Manteca	8 years	2 years/automatic unless nonrenewal notice is given

based on the amount of revenue generated or after stipulated periods of time.

Depending upon the terms of the agreement, newspapers may be provided a set payment for their editorial and administrative expenses, which is subtracted from revenues before revenues are divided as profit between the two firms. In other cases, newspapers receive only a share of revenue that must be used to cover their separate news and editorial expenses. Table 1.5 reports the terms for revenue distribution in existing JOAs.

Provisions for Losses

A variety of approaches have been taken in planning for the possibility of losses in JOAs (Table 1.6). In most cases, agreements stipulate that losses will be split according to owner interest in a joint firm or according to the formula used in dividing revenues.

Table 1.5. Revenue Division in JOAs

City	Revenue Division*
Albuquerque	*Journal* 60%, *Tribune* 40%
Birmingham	*News* 77.5%, *Post* 22.5%
Charleston	*Mail* 50%, *Gazette* 50%
Chattanooga	*News-Free Press*, 55%, *Times* 45%; slides to *News-Free Press* 70%, *Times* 30% based on revenue level
Cincinnati	*Enquirer* 60%, *Post* 40%; slides to *Enquirer* 80%, *Post* 20% based on revenue level
Detroit	*Free Press* 50%, *News* 50%
El Paso	*Times* 72.5%, *Herald-Post* 27.5%; slides to *Times* 75%, *Herald-Post* 25% after 1994
Evansville	*Press* 80%, *Courier* 20%; slides to *Press* 95%, *Courier* 5% based on revenue level
Fort Wayne	*News* 66.7%, *Journal-Gazette* 33.3%
Honolulu	*Star-Bulletin* 55%, *Advertiser* 45% (previously *Star-Bulletin* 80%, *Advertiser* 20%)
Las Vegas	*Review-Journal* 90%, *Sun* 10%
Miami	*Herald* 86%, Cox Newspapers 14%; slides to *Herald* 90%, Cox Newspapers 10% in 1993
Nashville	*Tennessean* 75.5%, *Banner* 24.5%; slides to *Tennessean* 83.5%, *Banner* 15.5% over length of contract
Pittsburgh	unavailable
Salt Lake City	*Tribune* 58%, *News* 42%
San Francisco	*Chronicle* 50%, *Examiner* 50%
Seattle	*Post-Intelligencer* 34%, *Times* 66%
St. Louis	*Post-Dispatch* 50%, Newhouse Newspapers 50%
Tucson	*Star* 50%, *Citizen* 50%
York	*Dispatch* 57.5%, *Record* 42.5%
	Joint Operations Not Covered by NPA
Lincoln	unavailable
Madison	Lee Enterprises 50%, Capital Times Co. 50%
	JOAs Ended
Anchorage	Advertising revenue split based on percentage of total circulation held using a sliding scale giving progressively higher amounts to the *Times*

18 JOINT OPERATING AGREEMENTS

Columbus	*Dispatch* approximately 75%, *Citizen-Journal* approximately 25%
Knoxville	*News Sentinel* 75%, *Journal* 25%
Oil City-Franklin	*Derrick* 50%, *News Herald* 50%
Shreveport	*Times* 79.5%, *Journal* 20.5%; slides to *Times* 81.5%, *Journal* 18.5% in 1994
Tulsa	*World* 60%, *Tribune* 40%
JOA Application Withdrawn	
Manteca	*Bulletin* 96%, *News* 4%

*After initial payments for management services, remuneration for unusual capital contributions or editorial costs

Most contracts have provisions that automatically terminate, or set up mechanisms for early termination of, JOAs if they result in losses. These typically provide that JOAs producing concurrent losses for two or three years will be ended and they stipulate the means for doing so.

Management

The management of the joint venture firm is placed in the hands of a board or committee established by the partners. The makeup of the committees varies, often favoring one partner over another as shown in Table 1.7.

The management of joint firms usually includes separate corporate boards and officers, which may or may not exercise operational management over the joint firm. Such boards typically provide more representation for the dominant newspaper. In some cases, the joint management is handed to officers or a management committee appointed by the board. In most cases these officers or committee members are disproportionately appointed based on control of the board and the joint firm. However, in some cases efforts are made to appoint an equal number representing each newspaper and then jointly pick an individual to represent the tie-breaking vote.

Table 1.6. Formulae For Covering Losses

City	Division of Losses
Albuquerque	*Journal* 60%, *Tribune* 40%
Birmingham	*News* 77.5%, *Post* 22.5%
Charleston	*Mail* 50%, *Gazette* 50%

Chattanooga	*News-Free Press*, 55%, *Times* 45%
Cincinnati	*Enquirer* 80%, *Post* 20%
Detroit	*Free Press* 50%, *News* 50%
El Paso	*Times* 72.5%, *Herald-Post* 27.5%; slides to *Times* 75%, *Herald-Post* 25% after 1994
Evansville	*Press* 80%, *Courier* 20%
Fort Wayne	*News* 66.7%, *Journal-Gazette* 33.3%
Honolulu	*Star-Bulletin* 55%, *Advertiser* 45%
Las Vegas	*Review-Journal* 90%, *Sun* 10%
Miami	*Herald* 100%
Nashville	*Tennessean* 75.5%, *Banner* 24.5%; slides to *Tennessean* 83.5%, *Banner* 15.5% over length of contract
Pittsburgh	unavailable
Salt Lake City	*Tribune* 58%, *News* 42%
San Francisco	*Chronicle* 50%, *Examiner* 50%
Seattle	*Post-Intelligencer* 34%, *Times* 66%
St. Louis	*Post-Dispatch* 50%, Newhouse Newspapers 50%
Tucson	*Star* 50%, *Citizen* 50%; slides to *Star* 55%, *Citizen* 45% based on amount of loss
York	*Dispatch* 57.5%, *Record* 42.5%

Joint Operations Not Covered by NPA

Lincoln	unavailable
Madison	Lee Enterprises 50%, Capitol Times Company 50%

JOAs Ended

Anchorage	unavailable
Columbus	unavailable
Knoxville	*News Sentinel* 75%, *Journal* 25%
Oil City-Franklin	*Derrick* 50%, *News Herald* 50%
Shreveport	*Times* 79.5%, *Journal* 20.5%; slides to *Times* 81.5%, *Journal* 18.5% in 1994
Tulsa	*World* 60%, *Tribune* 40%

JOA Application Withdrawn

Manteca	*Bulletin* 96%, *News* 4%

Table 1.7. Composition Of Joint Operation Management And Requirements For Decisions

City	Members Selected by Each Newspaper
Albuquerque	Policy Committee: 2 by *Journal*, 2 by *Tribune*. *Journal* is managing partner.
Birmingham	Management/Operations Committee: 3 by *News*, 2 by *Post*. Arbitrator used for disputes.
Charleston	Board: 2 by *Mail*, 2 by *Gazette*. Majority vote required for action; tie vote broken by managing director of American Newspaper Publishers Association.
Chattanooga	Operations Committee: 3 by *News-Free Press*, 2 by *Times*.
Cincinnati	*Enquirer* controls. No operations or policy committee specified.
Detroit	Board: 3 by *News*, 2 by *Free Press*. Majority vote required for action.
El Paso	*Times* controls.
Evansville	*Press* controls.
Fort Wayne	Board: 2 by *News*, 1 by *Journal-Gazette*. Officers: *News* selects President and Treasurer, *Journal-Gazette* selects Vice President.
Honolulu	Board: 2 by *Star-Bulletin*, 2 by *Advertiser*, 1 selected by both. Executive Committee: 2 by *Star-Bulletin*, 1 by *Advertiser*.
Las Vegas	*Review-Journal* controls. No operations or policy committee required. Quarterly meetings of "senior management" of both newspapers to discuss operations stipulated.
Nashville	Board: 5 members selected based on stockholders shares (*Tennessean* 70%, *Banner* 30%).
Pittsburgh	unavailable
Salt Lake City	Board: 2 by *Tribune*, 2 by *News*, 1 selected by both or by arbitration.
San Francisco	Structure gives each veto power over business decisions of other newspaper.
Seattle	Board: 3 by *Times*, 2 by *Post-Intelligencer*. Majority vote required for action.
Tucson	Board: 2 by *Star*, 2 by *Citizen*, 1 by both.
York	Board: 2 by *Dispatch*, 1 by *Record*. *Dispatch* selects chair.
Joint Operations Not Covered by NPA	
Lincoln	unavailable
Madison	Board: 5 by Lee Enterprises, 5 by Capital Times Co.
JOA Applications Withdrawn	
Manteca	*Bulletin* controls. No operations or policy committee stipulated. Arbitration used for disputes.

Similar types of management structures are created to handle JOAs where one newspaper acts as operating partner for both newspapers. When created, the management committees for these JOAs are comprised of managers of both newspapers, but control remains in the hands of the newspaper providing the services. The degree to which the control can be exercised is sometimes limited in the JOA contract, but that is not always the case.

Some agreements call for the use of arbitrators or neutral outsiders to be selected when conflicts occur between the representatives on the management board of the JOA newspapers. However, in most cases control is vested in the hands of a board weighted toward the dominant partner in the agreement. Where a majority vote is permitted to make decisions, this majority—if comprised of the representatives of the dominant partner—may make production and finance decisions over the objections of the second partner.

Market Allocation

Several major decisions regarding newspaper schedules and marketing are made during negotiations for a JOA. The partners decide which newspaper will be published in the morning and which in the evening, and whether or not to publish separate or combined weekend editions. In some cases, decisions are made about where each newspaper will circulate by determining who will publish statewide or regional editions.

THE EBB AND FLOW OF JOA NEWSPAPERS

JOAs do not guarantee the survival of their partners in perpetuity, primarily because they do not solve the problem of a disproportionate amount of advertising going to the newspaper with larger circulation. Thus, when a JOA agreement expires, the larger newspaper may choose not to renew the agreement if its dominance is so great that the other newspaper cannot survive on its own.

Since passage of the NPA in 1970, 16 newspapers have sought JOAs and 20 have dissolved such agreements or otherwise ceased publication (Tables 1.8 and 1.9).

Four particularly interesting occurrences are seen in Chattanooga, Anchorage, Knoxville, and Franklin-Oil City, PA. Chattanooga's two newspapers had a joint operation from 1942 until 1966, when the agreement was dissolved. In 1980, the newspapers decided to reenter the agreement and successfully applied to do so under the NPA. In 1974, the Anchorage newspapers formed a JOA, but dissolved their

22 JOINT OPERATING AGREEMENTS

Table 1.8. JOAs Sought Since Passage Of the Newspaper Preservation Act

City and Newspapers	Agreement Made	Approval Granted
Anchorage, AK News Times	1974	12-1-74
Chattanooga, TN News-Free Press Times	3-24-80	1-6-80
Cincinnati, OH Enquirer Post	9-23-77	11-26-79
Detroit, MI News Free Press	4-11-86	11-13-89
Las Vegas, NV Review-Journal Sun	7-12-89	6-1-90
Manteca, CA Bulletin News	1-25-88	withdrawn 9-11-91
Seattle, WA Post-Intelligencer Times	12-13-81	6-15-82
York, PA Dispatch Record	1-13-89	2-21-90

agreement four years later after bitter management differences. In 1990, the newspapers in Knoxville concluded an agreement to phase out their JOA, which had existed since 1957, over a two-year period. In 1985, the newspapers in the Franklin-Oil City JOA ended their agreement when one newspaper purchased the publishing company of the other newspaper and became the joint monopolist of the morning and evening newspapers.

There are two cases in which a JOA newspaper ceased publication but the JOA remains in force with the "dead" partner still receiving payments from the surviving partner. In Miami, Cox Enterprises continues to receive payments from Knight-Ridder even though its *Miami News* is no longer published. Similarly, the agreement between Newhouse Newspapers and the Pulitzer Company remains in force although the *St. Louis Globe-Democrat* is no longer published.

JOA operations that have ended, or that continue without publication of one of the partners, have typically had contracts of relatively short duration in which one partner dominated. The failed, or nonoperational, JOAs in Anchorage, Columbus, Miami, St. Louis, and Shreveport all operated under operating partner control in which the

Table 1.9. Joint Operations That Have Ceased Publication Or Ended

City and Newspapers	Comments
Anchorage, AK *Daily News* *Times*	Formed in 1974; dissolved in 1979; both newspapers are still publishing.
Bristol, VA *Herald-Courier* *Vir.-Tennessean*	Formed in 1950; combined in 1982; was joint monopoly rather than JOA; now a single all-day newspaper.
Chattanooga, TN *News-Free Press* *Times*	Formed in 1942; dissolved in 1966; reestablished JOA in 1980.
Columbus, OH *Citizen Journal* *Dispatch*	Formed 11-6-59; agreement expired 1985; *Dispatch* refused to renegotiate; *Citizen-Journal* closed
Knoxville, TN *News Sentinel* *Journal*	Formed in 1957; in 1990 the newspapers agreed to dissolve operations in 1992; *Journal* closed in 1992.
Miami, FL *Herald* *News*	Formed in 1966; renegotiated in 1988; News closed in 1988.
Oil City-Franklin, PA *Derrick* *News Herald*	Formed in 1956; *Derrick* purchased *News Herald* in 1985; now joint monopoly.
St. Louis, MO *Globe-Dispatch* *Post Dispatch*	Formed in 1959; dissolved 1984; *Globe-Democrat* sold, ceased publication in 1986.
Shreveport, LA *Times* *Journal*	Formed in 1953; dissolved early in 1991.
Tulsa, OK *World* *Tribune*	Formed in 1941; dissolved September 30, 1992; *Tribune* closed in 1992.

dominant newspaper had primary control over the operations of the secondary newspaper.

Operations in three other cities have mistakenly been thought to be JOAs. The Bristol, VA, *Herald-Courier* and *Virginia-Tennessean* were considered for a time to be a JOA when, in fact, they were a joint newspaper monopoly under the same ownership.

In 1986, the Department of Justice concluded that the JOAs in Madison, WI, and Lincoln, NE, were also joint monopolies. In these two cities, it was determined that the joint venture company rather than the individual publishing firms owned the two newspapers. The creation of the joint venture had been a merger rather than the creation of a traditional JOA (Leuders, 1987a, 1987b).

Thus, the ownership and operational structure of JOAs appear to have an influence on the ability of JOAs to serve their purported goal of preserving newspapers. When control is placed with one newspaper, the pursuit of its interests by its management can harm the JOA partner so that failure or termination of the agreement occurs.

2

Development of Joint Operations and the Newspaper Preservation Act

Three sets of significant events characterize the development of newspaper joint operations. The first phase consisted of the creation of individual joint operating agreements in several local markets starting in 1933. These agreements typically provided for the same cost-sharing, price-fixing, and profit-pooling arrangements found in current JOAs.

The second major event occurred when the U. S. Department of Justice obtained a summary judgment against the joint operation in Tucson, AZ, which was affirmed by the Supreme Court. This summary judgment permitted cost sharing between the Tucson newspapers, but found the price-fixing, profit-pooling, and market-allocation aspects of the joint operation to constitute an agreement in restraint of trade in violation of federal antitrust law. In effect, these illegal components of the challenged Tucson joint operation caused the two newspapers to function as a cartel, and this was not permitted in the Court's judgment. A cartel exists when two or more competitors agree to stop competing with each other in one or more areas such as pricing, level of output, fixing respective market shares, or granting exclusive product lines (e.g., one newspaper agrees to publish only in the morning while the other agrees to publish only in the afternoon).

This judicial action caused the third event to be set in motion. Newspaper companies involved in joint operations around the country

26   JOINT OPERATING AGREEMENTS

Table 2.1. Trends in Competitive Daily Newspaper Cities, 1880–1986

Year	Total Daily Cities	Cities with Competing Dailies	Percent of Total
1880	389	239	61.4%
1909–10	1,207	689	57.1
1920	1,295	552	42.6
1930	1,402	288	20.5
1940	1,426	181	12.7
1944–45	1,396	117	8.4
1953–54	1,448	87	6.0
1960	1,461	61	4.2
1968	1,500	45	3.0
1986	1,513	28	1.9

Sources: Reprinted by permission from "Trends in Daily Newspaper Ownership," by J.C. Busterna, 1988d, *Journalism Quarterly, 65*; "Trends in Daily Newspaper Ownership since 1945," by R.B. Nixon, 1954, *Journalism Quarterly, 31*; "Trends in U.S. Newspaper Ownership: Concentration with Competition," by R.B. Nixon, 1968, *Gazette, 14*(3).

successfully petitioned Congress to grant an exemption to the antitrust laws that would permit the restraints of trade in joint operations forbidden by the Court. The Newspaper Preservation Act, providing this exemption, was passed in 1970 and signed into law.

Each of these events will be described in turn. An important point to remember throughout this discussion is that the alternative to cartel JOAs permitted under the NPA need not be completely separate competitive newspapers. Before the NPA was passed, cost-sharing joint operations were permitted. They continued to be permitted after the Tucson case. The Tucson decision even permitted a cartel Sunday edition with shared profits and jointly set advertising and circulation rates, all before the NPA was put into law. These cost sharing joint operations should be considered as a policy alternative in addition to both seven-day-a-week cartel JOAs and fully separate competitive newspapers.

EARLY JOINT OPERATIONS

Throughout the 20th century, the daily newspaper industry has demonstrated a clear and continuous decline in the number of cities with competing newspapers. These numbers, presented in Table 2.1, suggest that if the joint operation is a successful way to preserve newspapers, it was not utilized much when it was most needed. In the 20 year period from 1910 to 1930, over 400 cities lost competing dailies. Yet, no joint operations were developed in any of these cities.

Daily newspaper joint operations only began after this period of declining competition. The *Albuquerque Journal* and *The New Mexico State Tribune* (now *The Albuquerque Tribune*) formed the first joint operation in 1933 ("JOA—A 50-Year Record," 1982).

Three other joint operations commenced before the end of the 1930s, in El Paso, Nashville, and Evansville. Of these first four joint operations, three involved newspapers owned by the Scripps-Howard chain, then the second largest newspaper company after Hearst. Notably, in a decade in which the overall number of cities with competing dailies dropped by 107, only four cities opted to form joint operations.

The joint operation strategy was successful in these early adoption markets because their pairs of newspapers are still currently publishing. Nevertheless, neither competitive newspaper was losing money in Evansville when the joint operation was begun in 1938 (Hearings on S. 1312, 1967, part 1, p. 265). One of these newspapers was (and still is) owned by Scripps-Howard. The president of Scripps-Howard in 1967, stated in Senate testimony that at the time the Evansville joint operation began company executives believed that competitive newspapers in medium-sized markets could not long remain competitive.

The 1940s was a quiet decade for the formation of new joint operations. New agreements began in Tucson and Tulsa before the onset of World War II. Papers in Madison, WI, formed the only other joint operation of the decade in 1948. The trend of the previous decade continued as fewer than 5% of cities that lost competing newspapers formed joint operations.

In testimony before Congress, publishers of newspapers in these cities contended that they faced inevitable failure without the formation of the competition-ending joint operations. William A. Small, Jr., owner of the *Tucson Citizen*, stated that collapse of his newspaper was inevitable because it carried substantial debt, had an overdrawn bank account, and had paid no dividends in many years (Hearings on S. 1312, Part 1, p. 6). However, in reviewing the Tucson situation before the joint operation was formed in 1940, the U.S. Supreme Court agreed with a lower court, finding that the *Citizen* was not a failing company (U.S. v. Citizen Publishing, 1968, p. 980; Citizen Publishing Co. v. U.S., 1969, p. 137).

Congressional testimony relating to these early joint operations was also characterized by the delicate avoidance of the price-fixing and profit-pooling aspects of these agreements. The testimony often made it appear that cost saving was the only motivation for these joint operations. Richard L. Jones, Jr., president of the Tulsa Tribune Company, said he "had seen and had studied the cost reductions in Albuquerque, El Paso, Nashville, and Tucson, where two separate newspapers had pooled facilities, equipment, and personnel into a one-plant operation and still preserved for their communities separate editorial voices and the rivalry and competitive spirit of their two news staffs" (Hearings on S. 1312, Part 1, p. 233).

By 1950, about 85% of the cities with competitive daily newspapers in 1910 had become cities with monopoly dailies (either single newspapers or two newspapers owned by the same company). Perhaps because the prospect of inevitable failure in most competitive markets became more of a reality, the creation of new joint operations picked up steam in the 1950s. Eleven new joint operations began during this decade out of the more than 40 cities that ceased to have competitive newspapers.

One of these joint operations was in Birmingham, AL. Again, a Scripps-Howard newspaper was involved. In testimony, an executive of the chain presented an altruistic reason for forming the joint operation: "The Birmingham joint arrangement entered into in 1950 seemed to us to offer the solution most favorable to the public interest, for it preserved two separate, independent newspapers" (Hearings on S. 1312, Part 1, p. 265). This statement appears dubious on at least two counts. First, it seems unlikely that Scripps-Howard based its decision in Birmingham on which option would best serve the public interest. The company's executives were more likely to be basing their decision on which option would generate the greatest profit. Forming a cartel appeared to be a good option to accomplish this. Second, we should be troubled by the proposition that by forming a cartel, two newspaper companies can remain separate and independent.

Of the 16 cities that lost daily newspaper competition from 1960 through 1968, four pairs of newspapers formed joint operations. These four markets—Pittsburgh, Honolulu, San Francisco, and Miami—were larger in population than the typical cities that had preceded them in forming joint operations. Competition had already died in nearly all smaller newspaper markets.

Between 1968 and 1986 there was a net loss of 17 cities with competitive daily newspapers. Newspapers in only two of these cities, Seattle and Cincinnati, chose to form JOAs. By 1990, the number of cities with competing dailies fell from 28 to 21. Newspapers in three of the seven cities that lost competing newspapers chose to form JOAs: Detroit, Las Vegas, and York.

When comparing these more recent years to the earlier part of the century, it is clear that the popularity of joint operation cartels increased significantly. If all the publishers of competitive daily newspapers in the earlier part of the century had the benefit of 20–20 hindsight, we might expect to have found more joint operations begun in the earlier time period.

However, another trend seems to be emerging. Although a higher proportion of competitive newspapers are entering into new JOAs, a growing number of existing JOAs have begun to break up. The Anchorage JOA broke up in 1979, Bristol in 1982, Columbus in 1985, Franklin-Oil City in 1985, St. Louis in 1986, Miami in 1988, Shreveport in 1991, Knoxville in 1991, Tulsa in 1992. So although there has been a trend toward a greater number of competing newspapers opting to form new JOAs, they still constitute a small minority of cities where newspaper competition has ceased (nine out of 40 since 1960 have formed new JOAs). Furthermore, since 1979, nine existing JOAs have ended.

In any event, 668 cities with competitive daily newspapers in 1910 lost that competition by 1990. In 1990, only 20 cities, about 3% of the original number of cities with competitive dailies, had daily newspapers with joint operating agreements under the Newspaper Preservation Act. Joint operations, even with the profit-enhancing benefit of cartel arrangements, have historically done a very poor job of preserving a second newspaper voice in most previously competitive newspaper cities.

THE CITIZEN PUBLISHING CASE

An abrupt change in the history of newspaper joint operations occurred in 1965 when the U.S. Department of Justice filed suit against the two joint operating daily newspapers in Tucson, AZ. The government charged the newspapers with two illegal activities. First, the government stated that the joint operation was a contract in restraint of trade in violation of Section 1 of the Sherman Act. Through this contract the two newspapers were said to be able to monopolize the daily newspaper market in Tucson in violation of Section 2 of the Sherman Act. The second charge was that the outright purchase of *The Arizona Evening Star* (hereinafter *Star*) by the stockholders of *The Tucson Daily Citizen* (hereinafter *Citizen*) was a merger in violation of Section 7 of the Clayton Act.

This government intervention may have caught elements of the newspaper industry by surprise, since there had previously been little antitrust activity directed against newspapers. Although the Sherman Act was passed in 1890, over 40 years lapsed before it was applied indirectly against newspapers in two Associated Press cases. Some of this reluctance may have been caused by the government's concern that the First Amendment protection of a free press precluded antitrust actions against newspapers. In 1937, in *Associated Press v. National Labor Relations Board*, the Supreme Court first declared that the

First Amendment does not protect newspapers from the antitrust laws:

> The business of the Associated Press is not immune from regulation because it is an agency of the press. The publisher of a newspaper has no special immunity from the application of general laws. He has no special privilege to invade the rights and liberties of others. He must answer for libel. He may be punished for contempt of court. He is subject to the antitrust laws. (p. 132)

In 1945, the Supreme Court spoke again, this time in language that could be interpreted as not permitting joint operations, although joint operations had nothing to do with the case. Indeed, Justice Douglas, writing the majority opinion in the Citizen Publishing case in 1969, which struck down the cartel aspects of joint operations, quoted this same passage. In *Associated Press v. United States*, Justice Black, writing for the majority stated,

> It would seem strange indeed...if the grave concern for freedom of the press which prompted adoption of the First Amendment should be read as a command that the government was without power to protect that freedom. The First Amendment, far from providing an argument against application of the Sherman Act, here provides powerful reasons to the contrary. That Amendment rests on the assumption that the widest possible dissemination of information from diverse and antagonistic sources is essential to the welfare of the public, that a free press is a condition of a free society. Surely a command that the government itself shall not impede the free flow of ideas does not afford nongovernmental combinations a refuge if they impose restraints upon that constitutionally guaranteed freedom. Freedom to publish is guaranteed by the Constitution, but freedom to combine to keep others from publishing is not. Freedom of the press from governmental interference under the First Amendment does not sanction repression of that freedom by private interests. The First Amendment affords not the slightest support for the contention that a combination to restrain trade in news and views has any constitutional immunity. (p. 20)

Thirty-two years had passed while the number of cartel joint operations had been allowed to grow without intervention by federal antitrust regulators. There may have been no intervention 1965 had the two joint operating daily newspapers in Tucson not attempted to merge.

In 1940, when the two separately owned daily newspapers entered into their joint operating agreement, the two owners agreed in writing that if either owner should desire to sell their newspaper in the future, the owners of the other newspaper would have a first refusal option to purchase (U.S. v. Citizen Publishing, 1968, p. 983). In 1964, the owners of the *Star* decided to sell and received a purchase offer from Brush-Moore Newspapers, Inc. The owners of the *Citizen* exercised their option to purchase the *Star*.

Although the joint operation had been allowed to function in Tucson for 25 years, it was only at the time of this merger that the U.S. Department of Justice intervened. Furthermore, the government had not attempted to block the joint operations in any of the other 20 markets where they were in force at the time the suit was brought in Tucson. Nor was Tucson the largest or oldest joint operation. The catalyst for the government intervention in Tucson was the fact that the two newspapers had merged.

As has already been noted, the Justice Department did not simply intervene to block the merger, though that appeared to be its motivation for taking any action. Indeed, the government asked for a summary judgment from the federal district court in Arizona on the grounds that the joint operation, begun in 1940, was a contract in restraint of trade, an issue separate from that of the merger of 1965. The district court was so certain that the joint operation was a contract in restraint of trade that it didn't even consider the issue worthy of trial. Summary judgment in favor of the government's claim was granted and affirmed later by the Supreme Court.

The case was tried on the other issues of whether the joint operation had the effect of monopolizing the daily newspaper market in Tucson, the charge regarding Section 2 of the Sherman Act; and whether the merger "may substantially lessen competition or tend to create a monopoly" in that market, the charge regarding Section 7 of the Clayton Act. Most of the *Citizen Publishing* case dealt with these monopolization issues. The case is one of only two Supreme Court cases to directly address the issue of what the relevant product and geographic market is for daily newspapers. That issue is dealt with more fully in Chapter 5.

Both the district court and Supreme Court decisions agreed on the facts of the case. Both the court decisions declared that the two Tucson newspapers competed vigorously prior to entering the joint operation in 1940. Their circulations were about equal, but the *Star* received about 50% more advertising revenue. The *Star* typically earned a small profit each year before the joint operation (about $26,000), while the *Citizen* incurred small yearly losses (about $24,000).

In 1936, Citizen Publishing was purchased for $100,000. At about that time, the new owners of the *Citizen* began discussions with Star Publishing to enter a joint operation. While these discussions continued, Citizen Publishing incurred $109,000 in debts from 1936 through 1939. Although these losses might suggest that the *Citizen* was a failing newspaper, neither the federal district court nor the Supreme Court could be convinced of this. Although neither decision suggested that the losses incurred by the *Citizen* while involved in talks to form a joint operation were not genuine, this idea has been suggested in several other joint operations. The appearance of losses just prior to a cartel agreement helps to justify the arrangement, but they may not have existed without the prospect of a cartel. Certainly, the operation of the cartel quickly makes up for any of these losses and the agreement in Tucson was no exception.

In the five years prior to the 1940 agreement, the combined profits of the *Star* and *Citizen* never exceeded 2.2 percent of revenues. In the first full year of the joint operation this rose to 10.4 percent. From 1940 through 1964, before-tax profits never fell below 10.2 percent in any year, and in the five years prior to the lawsuit, before-tax profits averaged 20 percent of revenues. Combined before-tax profits rose 6,174 percent from 1940 to 1964 (p. 982).

The Tucson joint operating agreement of 1940 stated that each newspaper would maintain separate news and editorial departments. The agreement also created Tucson Newspapers, Incorporated (TNI), a joint venture corporation owned equally by Citizen Publishing and Star Publishing. TNI had the responsibility of managing and operating all the other (non-news) departments that had previously been run separately by the two newspapers. The two publishing companies transferred about 90 percent of their equipment to TNI. TNI ran a single business department that was responsible for such things as the purchase of supplies, as well as maintaining personnel and other business records. TNI also operated a single composing room, a single stereotype department, combined printing press facilities, a dummy desk, and a proof room.

After subtracting its own expenses, TNI distributed the remaining advertising and circulation revenue to the two newspapers according to a preset formula. Each newspaper paid for its own news and editorial expenses out of this revenue share and kept the remainder for its profit. TNI set advertising and circulation prices for both newspapers. Lastly, Star Publishing and Citizen Publishing and their stockholders, officers, and executives all agreed they would not engage in any other publishing business in Tucson's Pima County.

The district court found that the joint operation of circulation, advertising, and production departments resulted in "substantial cost savings" (p. 982). The court also found that the agreement between the two newspapers called for jointly set advertising and circulation prices, profits to be pooled and distributed to the two newspapers according to a specified ratio, and a promise that the owners of the two newspapers would not compete with each other in any other business (pp. 980–981). The court agreed that some of the cost saving aspects could continue, but that the price fixing, profit pooling, and market allocation aspects of the agreement were *per se* violations of Section 1 of the Sherman Act. All these findings were affirmed by the Supreme Court.

On the subject of joint operations, the case was significant because the district court, affirmed later by the Supreme Court, allowed some aspects of the joint agreement to stand. The district court decision stated:

> The printing and distribution of *Star* and *Citizen* through joint use of substantially the same mechanical equipment does not depend upon the continuation of the price-fixing, profit-pooling, and market-allocation agreements. The restoration of competition to the daily newspaper business in Tucson requires that *Star* and *Citizen* have separate advertising departments and circulation departments. (pp. 992–993)

The decree of the district court, again affirmed by the Supreme Court, required the Tucson newspapers to modify their joint operation to eliminate price fixing, profit pooling, and market allocation. The modified, legal agreement permitted virtually all of the cost-saving aspects of the previous joint operation, including a jointly produced Sunday newspaper, and a combination advertising rate for the Monday through Saturday editions (U.S. v. Citizen Publishing Co., 1970, p. 88280).

This decision to allow the cost-saving aspects of the joint operation is even more remarkable in that both the district court and Supreme Court decisions did not require one of the newspapers in these joint operations to qualify as a failing firm. Indeed, both the district court and the Supreme Court decisions stated that neither Tucson newspaper was failing in 1940, at the time the joint operation was formed, nor in 1965, at the time of the government's suit. Yet, these decisions stated that the cost sharing aspects of the joint operation were still legal. This decision would have permitted any newspapers in the country to enter cost-sharing joint operations with their competitors without breaking any laws and without even needing the permission of the government. Ironically, the Newspaper Preservation Act requires one of the newspapers in a joint operation to be "failing," thus discouraging the cost-sharing, newspaper-preserving aspects of the *Citizen Publishing* agreement.

However, not much was made of this point by those who have analyzed the *Citizen Publishing* case. The primary concern raised by the decision focused on the issue of the failing firm defense. The failing firm issue was raised in the Supreme Court decision itself and has been the subject of many articles dealing with the case. This is undoubtedly because in his decision for the majority, Justice Douglas stated that the failing firm defense was the only possible means that the newspapers had to justify their cartel, and even this may not be sufficient (Citizen Publishing v. U.S., 1969, p. 136).

The failing firm defense consists of the proposition that the purchase of a competitive firm is not a violation of antitrust law when the acquired company is in a failing financial condition. The first case to allow a merger on the basis of the failing firm defense under the Sherman Act was *American Press Association v. United States* in 1917, in which the two remaining firms in a market were allowed to merge because one was soon to fail at any rate. Later cases at the Supreme Court level acknowledged the legitimacy of the defense under the antimerger provision of Section 7 of the Clayton Act (International Shoe Co. v. FTC, 1930; Brown Shoe Co. v. United States, 1962).

All of these cases and articles dealt with the failing firm defense in the context of a merger that might otherwise violate the Sherman Act or Section 7 of the Clayton Act. Justice Douglas was, therefore, not sure whether the defense would even be applicable to the cartel aspects of the joint operation in the *Citizen Publishing* case because these issues were not affected by the merger. It does appear reasonable that if a merger involving a firm that would otherwise fail should be permitted, then the same logic should apply to cartel operations.

This point was made many times by the proponents of joint operating cartels during the Newspaper Preservation Act hearings. However, the *per se* doctrine of Section 1 of the Sherman Act regarding restraint of trade cases might upset this logic. Merger cases are supposed to be handled by a "rule of reason" that may find some mergers reasonable if they do not reduce competition or provide counterbalancing benefits to the decline in competition. On the other hand, restraint of trade cases involving price fixing and profit pooling (typically found in newspaper joint operations) are governed by a *per se* rule. Under the *per se* doctrine, practices are illegal regardless of whether they are shown to have antisocial effects or not (U.S. v. Trans-Missouri Freight, 1897, p. 328).

In any case, Justice Douglas found the failing firm defense applicability on the cartel charges moot because he agreed with the lower court that Citizen Publishing was not a failing firm. Justice Douglas found that there was no evidence that the owners of the *Citizen* were considering going out of business. The owners never sought to sell the paper. There was no evidence that the joint operation was "the last straw at which the *Citizen* grasped." The *Citizen* was considered by the Court to be a significant threat to the *Star*. The Court ruled that the failing firm defense cannot be applied when it is not first established that the competitor was the only available purchaser (Citizen Publishing v. U.S., 1969, pp. 137–138).

Justice Stewart wrote a strong dissent centered on the issue of the failing firm defense. He stated that the district court judge had erred in thinking that the defense did not apply in Sherman Act Section 1 cases. He disagreed with the majority and argued that because the newspapers did not submit the evidence requested by the majority after the trial was held, the *Citizen* must not be considered as failing. Had the newspapers known of the new evidence requirements established by the Supreme Court in the *Citizen Publishing* case, they might have been able to demonstrate them to the Court's satisfaction. Thus, Justice Stewart argued the case should be remanded back to the lower court to be reheard on this new standard on the failing firm (Citizen Publishing v. U.S., 1969, pp. 143–146).

As a result of this exchange, the debate that has arisen over the *Citizen Publishing* decision, and later the Newspaper Preservation Act, has focused on what constitutes a failing firm. Although this is an important concern in determining whether a defense exists for the operation of a joint operating cartel, it quickly turned the subsequent analysis away from the option of competitive, non-cartel joint operations. These were permitted even under the tough failing firm definition in the *Citizen Publishing* case, since that decision permitted competitive joint operations even between two very profitable competitors.

Thus, this Supreme Court decision and the resulting modified joint operating agreement in Tucson could have been viewed as a great opportunity for competing newspapers throughout the country to immediately form cost-sharing joint operations even (or especially) while both newspapers were financially healthy and profitable. Thus, quite a few competitive newspapers that have ceased publication or merged since the late 1960s could have been preserved to this day. Instead, the response to the *Citizen Publishing* case got sidetracked on the failing firm issue. As a result, much of the newspaper industry petitioned Congress to provide for an antitrust exemption to allow price fixing and profit pooling cartels.

THE NEWSPAPER PRESERVATION ACT

The Newspaper Preservation Act was signed into law in 1970, but it began its legislative history on 1967 as the Failing Newspaper Act. Senate bill 1312, the Failing Newspaper Act, was cosponsored by 15 senators. This legislation was introduced after the district court had ruled the cartel aspects of joint operations in the *Citizen Publishing* case to be in violation of the Sherman Act, but before the Supreme Court affirmed that decision or the district court had modified the Tucson joint operation. The hearings continued in both houses of Congress through various sessions ending October 1, 1969.

The leading force behind the early legislative effort was Senator Carl Hayden (R-AZ). Hearings on S. 1312 were held from July 12, 1967, to April 16, 1968. After the first set of hearings in 1967, Senator Daniel K. Inouye (D-HI) (where another pair of joint operating newspapers were published) became the chief sponsor of S. 1520, The Newspaper Preservation Act, which replaced S. 1312. Hearings on S. 1520 ran from June 12–June 20, 1969.

In the House, one of the chief proponents of the NPA was Representative Spark Matsunaga (D-HI). Hearings on H. R. 19123 were held from September 18–October 3, 1968. Hearings were continued in the next Congress under bill H. R. 279 from September 10–October 1, 1969. Nearly all the cosponsors of the bills related to the NPA were either from states that had joint operating newspapers or from states that had nonjoint operating newspapers belonging to chains that had joint operating newspapers. Clearly, the Failing Newspaper Act, and later the Newspaper Preservation Act, were responses by members of Congress to a powerful special interest group.

The hearings in the Senate and the House generated over 5,000 pages of printed testimony and exhibits given over a two-year period. Yet, the crucial issue of the hearings was raised by the first speaker on the first day, William A. Small Jr., owner of the *Tucson Citizen*. He stated that separate staffing of the advertising and circulation departments "would eliminate many of the economies which brought the papers together in the first place" (Hearings on S. 1312, p. 9). He also stated that a shared Sunday edition was crucial to the survival of the *Citizen* (Hearings on S. 1312, p. 9). Without a Sunday edition the *Citizen* would go out of business. The alternative of operating a second set of presses and delivery trucks to accommodate a second Sunday morning newspaper would eliminate most of the remaining cost savings of joint operation.

The Department of Justice was steadfastly opposed to the passage of the act throughout the hearings, but they were willing to support most of the requests of William Small and other owners of joint operating newspapers. Representatives of the Justice Department told both congressional subcommittees to wait until the case was resolved in the courts including whatever modified agreement the district court would approve in Tucson. The Justice Department argued that by waiting until the final decree was published, Congress could then better understand if there was still a need for the NPA. The Department made it clear during the hearings that virtually all the cost savings available under the NPA would be available without it (Hearings on H. R. 279, p. 359).

Congress did not take this advice and passed the NPA shortly before the district court published the modified agreement for the joint operating newspapers in Tucson (U.S. v. Citizen Publishing, 1970, p. 88280). The agreement between the Department of Justice and the Tucson newspapers allowed for a jointly produced Sunday newspaper. Both newspapers in the modified joint operation agreement would share the cost and revenue of the Sunday newspaper and jointly set Sunday advertising and circulation rates just as JOA newspapers under the NPA. The modified agreement also allowed the two Tucson newspapers to sell combination ads during the rest of the week. Each newspaper was required to independently determine their own rate card, but they agreed upon cost-justified combination rates.

The Tucson agreement further stipulated that a merged sales staff could sell Sunday and daily combination advertising. However, Sunday and daily combination advertising constituted nearly all the advertising that was sold by the two newspapers when they operated for five months in 1970 under the court-imposed modified agreement before the NPA was enacted. Emil Rould, secretary of Tucson Newspapers, Inc., recalled in a telephone conversation of August 5, 1990, to one of the authors that each newspaper had only one salesperson to handle advertising that was daily noncombination during the five-month period.

Thus, without the NPA, the Tucson newspapers got virtually all they asked for in terms of cost saving. Virtually all the cost sharing considerations such as printing, distribution, bookkeeping, and so on, were either identical, or nearly so, between the modified agreement and the provisions of the NPA. Price fixing and profit pooling were allowed on Sunday because the Department of Justice agreed that each newspaper needed Sunday revenue to be profitable.

The only significant difference between the modified non-NPA agreement in Tucson and JOA provisions that are permitted under the NPA is that the Department of Justice did not allow price fixing and profit pooling for the Monday through Saturday editions. No person ever testified that without the ability to have a Monday through Saturday cartel, joint operating newspapers would fail. William Small's first day testimony had only asked for combined advertising and circulation staffs and a cartel Sunday edition. The non-NPA agreement at the resolution of the *Citizen Publishing* case gave him all these things.

During the hearings, many people spoke in favor of the NPA legislation and many spoke against it. However, none of the testimony (except some vague suggestions and warnings from the Department of

Justice) provided in the two years of hearings addresses the actual policy choice that was faced by Congress. All other testimony assumed that there were only two alternatives to cartel JOAs: totally separate operation or sharing of only printing and distribution. Congress was apparently convinced that neither alternative would be enough to preserve second newspapers.

NPA supporters typically argued that joint operations were needed to reduce costs, but never explained why price fixing and profit pooling were the solution to the cost problems facing two separately owned newspapers in a local market. See, for example, the testimony of Arthur B. Hanson, General Counsel, American Newspaper Publishers Association, or Representative Matsunaga (Hearings on S. 1312, 1967, part 1, p. 51, and Hearings on H. R. 279, 1969, pp. 15–22). This problem is compounded because proponents never were confronted with the need to argue that the NPA was necessary for its incremental effects over the modified Tucson agreement (principally the Monday through Saturday price fixing and profit pooling).

NPA opponents typically argued that the failure of a second newspaper was not such a terrible thing. Opponents often believed that failure was caused by poor management or by a preference for one newspaper over another by readers and advertisers. Senator Hart, one of the members of the subcommittee holding the NPA hearings, asked, "Would it have been better still if a new fellow had been free to move in after the disappearance of the sickly one and really do the job, and could that ever happen if we pass a bill like this and guarantee the existence of the less vigorous of the two in the community?" (Hearings on S. 1312, part 1, p. 69). Senator Hart, who went on to oppose the NPA, did not realize at the time that this was an irrelevant point. Whether the NPA was passed or not, the stronger newspaper in a market could form a joint operation that would keep the weaker newspaper in business and make it as good as impossible for a third newspaper to enter.

Even two years later, near the end of the hearings, but before the Tucson modified agreement had been released, the same shortcoming existed. Stephen Barnett, law professor at the University of California, testifying against the legislation, argued that a JOA under the NPA would constitute a government charter that would grant newspaper publishing rights to two companies in a cartel as a deterrent against any other newspapers entering the market (Hearings on H. R. 279, pp. 243–244). Again, even without passage of the NPA, the modified Tucson agreement showed that all the essential aspects of joint operation under the NPA would be permitted without it, except for the requirement that the two newspapers compete Monday through

Saturday. This would still create a virtually insurmountable barrier to any potential entrant.

Indeed, neither the proponents nor the opponents of the NPA could have known the alternative to the NPA during the hearings. Even near the end of the two years of hearings, Richard W. McLaren, head of the Antitrust Division of the Justice Department, testified that he opposed allowing a joint advertising sales force even though he favored a joint combination rate and a cartel on Sunday (Hearings on H. R. 279, p. 359, p. 362). This still suggested that some significant cost saving could result by passage of the NPA because it would eliminate the need to have two redundant sales forces. When the modified Tucson agreement was put into place a few months after the hearings, only one salesperson overlapped at each newspaper.

Whereas the usefulness of the Congressional hearings was destroyed by the failure to wait for the modified Tucson joint operation, law review articles on the NPA also suffer from a failure to acknowledge the modified agreement. Many of these articles, which criticized and offered alternatives to the NPA, were written before the modified agreement was reached. Others did not acknowledge the contents of the modified agreement, perhaps because the document itself was not included in the district court's final report (U.S. v. Citizen Publishing, 1970, p. 88280).

As a result of writing before the agreement was reached, or ignoring it in the later articles, the best alternative to JOAs under the NPA was never presented. Most of these articles opposed the NPA. Typically, they argued that making an exception in the antitrust laws was a bad idea, or that letting fully separated newspapers compete in the marketplace was a better alternative (Barnett, 1989; Barwis, 1980; Becker, 1970; Carlson, 1971; Carlson, 1982; Gibboney, 1971; Martel & Haydel, 1984; Patkus, 1984; Roberts, 1968; Robinson, 1979).

Opponents of the NPA did not need to make such a strong case. The alternative to the NPA, complete with a Sunday cartel and daily combination rate sold by a single advertising sales force, is not very different than the NPA itself. Indeed, Wright (1969) lamented this fact over 20 years ago. He believed that the Department of Justice and the Court gave the Tucson newspapers too much leeway.

Proponents of the NPA also do injustice to the policy debate when they claim that the alternative to the NPA is fully separated competing newspapers. Lacy (1990a) argues that "a high probability exists that all of the current JOA markets would lose one of their two papers if the Newspaper Preservation Act were repealed" (p. 3). However, this conclusion assumes that these newspapers would face full competition if the NPA were repealed. The proponents of the NPA must argue instead that allowing a Monday through Saturday cartel is the only factor that would prevent the weaker newspaper in each JOA city from failing. After all, this is the only significant advantage that a joint operation under the NPA allows over joint operations functioning without the NPA.

3
Application of the Newspaper Preservation Act

The Newspaper Preservation Act specifies that a joint operating agreement covered under it may be established only "with prior written consent of the Attorney General of the United States" and that the consent can be provided only after a determination by the U.S. Attorney General that one of the papers is a failing newspaper (15 U. S. C. 1803(b)).

In order to implement this part of the NPA, Attorney General John Mitchell proposed a variety of procedures and rules to provide public notice and give his department and the public information on which to respond to applications (Fed. Reg. 20435 (1971)). The rules immediately led to disputes over provisions requiring applicants to provide financial information and to publish notices that they were applying for a JOA (Huston, 1972; Keep, 1982). Publishers argued that the data would reveal proprietary business data and that the requirement of publication violated the rights of publishers to determine what they would publish. Despite the opposition of the publishers and the American Newspaper Publishers Association, the rules were not substantially altered.

In its interim rules, the Attorney General's office stated that publishers need not obtain its approval for a joint operating agreement if they did not intend to violate existing antitrust statutes and did not wish to go through the approval procedures to obtain the NPA exemption (Fed. Reg. 7 (1974)). The rule led to a legal challenge by the Newspaper Guild, which argued that it contradicted the language of the NPA. Although a U.S. District Court sided with the Guild (Newspaper Guild v. Saxbe, 1974), the U.S. Court of Appeals upheld the regulation, saying the NPA did not make joint operations unlawful but provided a means for existing and future joint operations to receive the antitrust exemption (Newspaper Guild v. Levi, 1977).

Thus, publishers who wish to enter a JOA that does not involve price fixing, profit pooling, and other anticompetitive acts may do so without seeking approval and without the necessity of proving that one newspaper is failing (Keep, 1982; Patkus, 1984).

However, publishers who wish to apply for the antitrust exemption under the NPA must seek approval and show that one newspaper meets the "failing newspaper" test. The Attorney General's regulations, codified in 1976 in 28 C. F. R. 48.1-48.16, specify the processes and internal guidelines used today for handling and analyzing JOA applications.

The guidelines provide that although the Attorney General has the decision-making responsibility, he or she may delegate that responsibility to others in the Justice Department, except for persons in the Antitrust Division who are asked to provide an independent analysis.

When an application is filed, a notice of its receipt is published in the *Federal Register* and a 30-day period is specified for receipt of written comments on whether the application should be approved, disapproved, or if a public hearing should be held to determine matters of fact. The U.S. Attorney General can, at his discretion, extend this and other time periods in order to facilitate inquiry by acquiring additional evidence or analysis. Figure 3.1 provides an overview of the application and administrative process.

During the comments period, the Antitrust Division undertakes a study of the application and other relevant materials with the intent of producing a report on the situation and a recommended course of action for the Attorney General. During the inquiry, the antitrust officials may request additional evidence and documentation from the applicants, commission research, and seek expert advice. Once the division submits its report, a second 30-day comments period follows in order for interested parties to respond to the report or enter other comments.

After these comments, the Attorney General decides whether to approve or disapprove the application, or to order hearings to gather additional information. Should a hearing be ordered, the assistant Attorney General for Administration appoints an administrative law judge for that purpose. When hearings are held, the report and recommendations of the Antitrust Division are considered and the division participates in the hearings, along with the applicants. Other interested groups and individuals, such as employees and community groups, may petition the Attorney General to intervene.

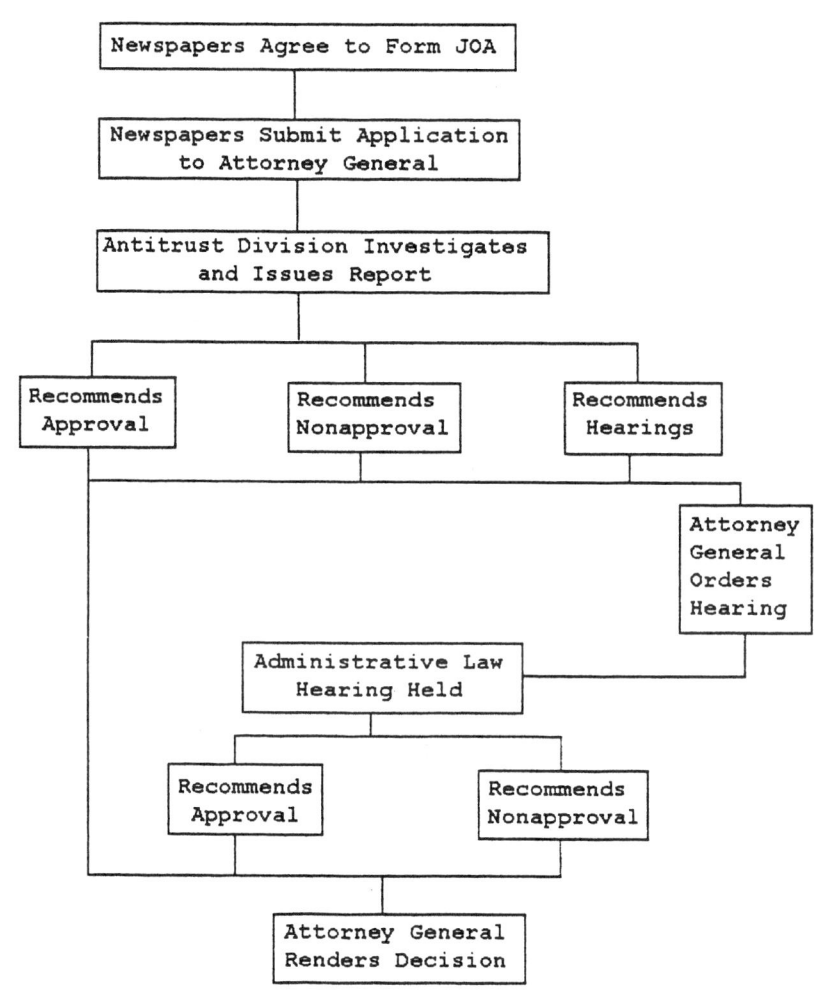

APPLICATION OF THE NEWSPAPER PRESERVATION ACT 43

```
Newspapers Agree to Form JOA
            │
Newspapers Submit Application
       to Attorney General
            │
Antitrust Division Investigates
       and Issues Report
            │
   ┌────────┼────────┐
Recommends  Recommends  Recommends
 Approval   Nonapproval  Hearings
                            │
                       Attorney
                       General
                       Orders
                       Hearing
                            │
              Administrative Law
                 Hearing Held
                      │
              ┌───────┴───────┐
          Recommends       Recommends
           Approval        Nonapproval
                      │
              Attorney General
              Renders Decision
```

Figure 3.1. Process For Gaining JOA Approval

After hearings are held, the administrative law judge prepares a recommended decision that is forwarded to the Attorney General. Hearing participants may file post-hearing briefs with the Attorney General as well. After consideration of the recommendations and briefs, the Attorney General renders a decision.

APPLICATIONS SINCE PASSAGE OF THE NPA

Since the NPA went into effect, eight applications for approval of JOAs have been made to the Attorney General. The applications presented a different array of issues and facts to be considered.

This section will briefly describe the applicants, issues, and decisions in each case in chronological order. An overview will be provided of the development of the definitions and interpretations placed on the NPA and procedures by the Attorney General, administrative law judges, and federal courts. Subsequent sections will explore the importance and implications of the cases on the NPA and its operation.

Anchorage

The application of the *Anchorage Daily News* and *Times* to form the first post-NPA joint operation was made in 1974, four years after passage of the NPA. The *Daily News*, the morning newspaper that was designated the failing newspaper, lagged far behind its competitor in printing technology, circulation, and advertising.

The Anchorage Typographical Union had requested a hearing and public review of the finances of the two newspapers. However, the Antitrust Division's review satisfied the assistant attorney general, who recommended that Attorney General William Saxbe approve the application, with the stipulation that one provision that required preservation of each newspapers' existing quality and character be removed because it affected editorial matters that the NPA required be kept out of JOAs ("Preservation Act Ruled Cited," 1974). The newspapers agreed to the change and the pact was approved on December 1, 1974.

However, within two years it was evident that the joint operation was not financially aiding the *Daily News*, mainly because of unfavorable requirements for capital investments and profit allocation based on circulation performance (Hein, 1976; Keep, 1982).

The newspapers ultimately became opponents in litigation over the *Times*' operations on behalf of the *Daily News* and disputes over payments for services. In an out-of-court settlement, the newspapers agreed to disband the JOA as of March 21, 1979, and to drop their litigation, thus making their JOA not only the first to receive approval but the first to cease operating ("Anchorage Dailies to End Joint Agreement in April," 1978).

Cincinnati

In September 1977, the *Enquirer* and the *Post* came to an agreement to form a JOA after nearly five years of discussion. The afternoon newspaper, the *Post*, was designated the failing newspaper.

In February 1978, the Attorney General ordered that hearings be held, marking the first time the process was employed. Unions representing workers at the newspapers and a suburban newspaper publisher were granted the right to intervene in the case and hearings were held in September and October of that year.

During the hearings, much discussion focused on whether or not the *Post* had been mismanaged, whether all the expenses reported by management should be used as indicators of failure, and whether a search for a buyer of the *Post* should be required.

The administrative law judge found merit in the arguments that mismanagement might be a relevant factor, agreed with arguments that some costs should not be included in the determination of whether the *Post* was a failing newspaper, and accepted arguments that alternative solutions, such as the sale of the newspaper, must be explored. Although he found relevance in the arguments, he ruled that the record did not reveal significant mismanagement, that even with disputed cost removed the *Post* was still a failing newspaper, and that there was no evidence that the sale of the newspaper would be likely or improve the situation if a sale did occur. As a result, he recommended that the agreement be approved (Moore, 1979). The Attorney General approved the application in October 1978.

Chattanooga

The March 24, 1980, application of the *Times* and the *News-Free Press* to form the third new JOA was particularly intriguing because it involved two newspapers that had a joint operation formed in 1942 and dissolved in 1966 (Consoli, 1980).

In an effort to speed the joining of their operations, the newspapers also asked for temporary approval prior to a full decision by the Attorney General, a request that drew a negative recommendation from the Antitrust Division ("Papers Joint Operations Opposed in Justice Department," 1980) and was denied by Attorney General Benjamin Civiletti ("Civiletti Denies Request By Chattanooga Papers," 1980).

In a move that surprised many observers because of its lack of political sensitivity, the *Times* and *News-Free Press* did not wait for the decision and began joint operations anyway the day prior to the ruling. That decision induced the Antitrust Division to respond by recommending that the Attorney General deny approval of the entire application ("Antitrust Unit Opposes Chattanooga Paper Plan," 1980).

However, Civiletti asked the Antitrust Division to continue its full consideration of the application and to determine whether or not it would have recommended approval without the early establishment of joint operation. When its investigation was completed, the Antitrust

Division reported that it would have recommended approval if the newspapers had waited ("Antitrust Report Issued on Chattanooga Papers," 1980). Consequently, the division recommended providing approval only for portions of the joint activities that had not yet been implemented.

Attorney General Civiletti followed that recommendation on November 6, 1980, excluding some elements from the approval because they had begun early: the joint printing operation, discontinuance of the Sunday *Times*, and switch of the *News-Free Press* from Saturday morning to Saturday afternoon publication ("2 Papers in Chattanooga Given Partial Immunity," 1980).

The lack of approval for joint printing was not particularly significant because such activities typically did not violate antitrust provisions and could be entered into without approval by the Attorney General according to the *Newspaper Guild v. Levi* ruling. The agreements to divide the newspaper markets on Saturday and Sunday, however, placed the newspapers in antitrust jeopardy because they were not exempted. Nevertheless, the Justice Department chose not to pursue the case.

Seattle

A pact to join the morning *Post-Intelligencer* and the afternoon *Times* in a JOA was reached by the Hearst Corporation and the Seattle Times Company on January 13, 1981, and an application for approval was filed with the Attorney General on March 27, 1981. The Antitrust Division opposed granting approval to the application and recommended on May 27 that hearings be held. The Attorney General ordered the hearings in August, 1981.

Several citizens' groups and suburban newspaper publishers petitioned to intervene in the hearings and approval was granted. Hearings were held in Seattle throughout November focusing on a few key issues: whether adjusted expenses of the failing newspaper, the *Post-Intelligencer*, really indicated that it was failing; whether improvements in circulation indicated that the newspaper was no longer in a downward spiral; what could have been done, or could still be done, to improve the *Post-Intelligencer*'s position; and whether there were available purchasers for the newspaper.

The administrative law judge found that neither financial adjustments over disputed costs nor improvements in circulation during the application period warranted denial of the application. Although recognizing that deliberate mismanagement practices or decisions would be relevant to the determination of failure, he found nothing to suggest that such had taken place. He noted that at times, through tax advantages and other transfers, the *Post-Intelligencer* had been beneficial to its owner. However, he ruled that such benefits were irrelevant because of the NPA's wording that ownership of failing newspapers was not relevant.

The judge found that a variety of prospective purchasers existed as an alternative to the JOA and that the Hearst newspaper "could in all probability be sold at fair market value to a person or firm who could, and would, continue it in operation as an independent metropolitan daily" (Hanscom, 1982, p. 84). Unlike Judge Moore in the Cincinnati case, Judge Hanscom ruled that nothing in the NPA or its legislation required an owner to attempt to sell the newspaper before seeking a JOA and completely dismissed its relevancy.

The judge then recommended approval of the JOA on January 14, 1982, and Attorney General William French Smith approved the application on June 15, 1982. Although generally accepting the judge's decision, Smith stated that the availability of a potential purchaser might be relevant in determining the condition and prospects of a newspaper ("Opinion and Order," 1982, p. 11).

The decision set off a storm of controversy and arguments about whether the decision served or harmed the purposes of the NPA (Carlson, 1982; Martel & Haydel, 1984). The interveners in the case launched litigation to overturn the decision, the first judicial challenge of the decision of an administrative law judge and the Attorney General.

The U.S. District Court sided with the interveners, granting a summary judgment that overturned the Attorney General's order. The judge ruled that the Attorney General had ignored offers to purchase the newspaper and that Judge Moore's view of alternative solutions should be adopted (Committee for an Independent *Post-Intelligencer* v. Smith, 1982).

The District Court's ruling, however, was overturned in April, 1983 by the Court of Appeals, which accepted the general view promulgated by Judge Moore in the Cincinnati case, saying "alternatives to a JOA are relevant to the determination that a newspaper qualifies under the Act," but ruled that the *Post-Intelligencer*'s owners had provided sufficient evidence to indicate that a different owner could not solve the newspaper's problems. The court ruled that to halt a JOA the burden would be on opponents to show that losses were not irreversible, that management practices were unreasonable, or that other alternatives indicated a newspaper was not in danger of failure (Committee for an Independent *Post-Intelligencer* v. Hearst Corp., 1983).

The court ruled that the NPA itself was constitutional and that financial benefits accruing to a failing newspaper's owner, that ownership itself, and that potential harm to suburban competitors were irrelevant in determining whether approval of JOAs should be granted. Although interveners appealed the decision, the Supreme Court declined to review the Appeals Court decision.

Detroit

The application to form the fifth post-NPA joint operation generated the most interest and press coverage of any application in part because it would be the largest JOA and the newspapers were in the tightest competition ever seen in an application. Neither newspaper dominated the market, splitting it nearly in half. The *News* had a slight lead in circulation and advertising, which was eroding at the time of the application. The *Free Press*, which was gaining in both circulation and advertising, was named the failing newspaper.

The agreement was completed by the newspapers on April 11, 1986, and an application filed with the Attorney General on May 9. The Antitrust Division completed its review on July 23, 1986, indicating that the newspapers had not provided sufficient evidence that the *Free Press* was a failing newspaper and that significant questions were left unanswered: whether a downward circulation spiral existed, and whether expenditures for new printing facilities and an aggressive marketing campaign to become the dominant newspaper in Detroit should be counted as losses. The division recommended that hearings be held to resolve the issues (Ginsburg, 1986). Hearings were ordered by the Attorney General on February 25, 1987.

Hearings were held during August, 1987. Intervention by unions representing employees at the newspapers, suburban newspaper publishers, and citizens was approved and they took part in the proceedings.

Administrative Law Judge Morton Needelman submitted his report on December 29, 1987, recommending that the application for the JOA be denied. He stated that the *Free Press* was not dominated by the *News*, that it was not in a downward circulation spiral, that no prospects that a spiral would develop were shown, and that "losses incurred by the *Free Press* and *News* are attributable to their strategies of seeking market dominance and future profitability at the cost along with the expectation that failure to achieve these goals would result in favorable consideration of a JOA application" (Needelman, 1987, pp. 128–129).

Knight-Ridder, owner of the *Free Press*, and Gannett Co., owner of the *News*, began an aggressive campaign, lobbying Attorney General Edwin Meese to ignore the recommendation. On August 8, 1988,

Meese approved the joint operation despite the recommendations of the administrative law judge and his own Antitrust Division (Garneau, 1988).

Interveners in the case filed suit to overturn Meese's decision on the grounds that it was not based on evidence and it violated normal administrative law procedures. The U.S. District Court (Michigan Citizens for an Independent Press v. Attorney General of the United States, 1988) and Court of Appeals (Michigan Citizens for an Independent Press v. Attorney General of the United States, 1989) backed the attorney general's power in the matter, and the Supreme Court reached a stalemate on the matter with a 4–4 vote, allowing the JOA approval to stand (Michigan Citizens for an Independent Press v. Thornburgh, 1989).

Manteca

The most unusual application for a JOA began with the agreement of the *Bulletin* and *News* to form a joint operation on January 25, 1988. The papers filed their application on July 13, 1988.

The application was unusual because the agreement involved a daily newspaper, the *Bulletin*, and a semi-weekly publication, the *News*. In addition, the parties were not particularly amiable in their approach to the agreement, having previously been involved in predatory pricing litigation in which the *News* lost a jury verdict in a $6.3 million suit by the *Bulletin* (Stein, 1988). Disputes between the two continued. The JOA application even indicated that the JOA was a means to settle those disputes and that the *Bulletin* would file another lawsuit if the application was rejected ("Application for Approval of *Manteca News/Manteca Bulletin* Joint Newspaper Operating Arrangement," 1988, p. 11).

The investigation of the Antitrust Division was stymied by continuing disputes between the parties and delays in providing information. Despite the problems, the Attorney General granted extensions to the parties to keep the application alive. Finally, on August 13, 1990, the Antitrust Division issued a harsh recommendation that the application should be disapproved, saying that the *News* had not been shown to be failing, that it was not in a circulation spiral, and that poor management practices were the cause of its distress. The division also recommended that no hearings be held (Shaffert, 1990).

On November 2, 1990, Attorney General Richard Thornburgh rejected the division's recommendations against a hearing and ordered them to be held. The Antitrust Division began preparing for those hearings by taking depositions and conducting interviews in the spring of 1991. After its new investigation, the division reversed itself and recommended that the JOA be approved and that no hearings be held. The move led to a wave of protests among JOA opponents who questioned the division's turnabout on its original findings (Picard, 1991).

Numerous public comments on the division's new report were submitted to the Justice Department, many of which challenged the process and the decision to reverse without hearings. A decision on the matter was further delayed when Thornburgh left office in August to run for a U.S. Senate seat in Pennsylvania. Before the acting Attorney General could rule on the application, however, the *News* decided to close down rather than continue the process. On August 21, 1991, it published its final issue and withdrew its application for JOA approval.

York

The *Daily Record* and *Dispatch* agreed to form a JOA on January 13, 1989, and filed an application with the Attorney General on February 22.

The newspapers were located in one of the smallest communities in the nation to have competing dailies. The *Daily Record* trailed the *Dispatch* in both advertising and circulation sales and had a history of financial losses.

The Antitrust Division in June recommended approval without a hearing, despite the efforts of the York Citizens Independent Newspapers Committee to be heard (Boudin, 1989). Attorney General Richard Thornburgh approved the application on February 21, 1990, saying that its financial losses appeared irreversible, that attempts to sell were unsuccessful (Garneau, 1990a), and that the citizens' group had not raised issues that would materially effect the decision in the matter.

Las Vegas

On June 12, 1989, the *Sun* and the *Review-Journal* agreed to form a joint operation and applied for approval. Like the *Anchorage News*, the *Sun* was clearly disadvantaged and had only about a third of the circulation of its competitor.

Some observers were surprised that the *Review-Journal*'s owners agreed to enter the agreement because the *Sun* was in such poor condition that it would not have remained a competitor for long. Some unusual terms in the agreement, however, made the deal desirable. In agreeing to enter the JOA, the *Sun*'s owner agreed to give Donrey, the

Review-Journal's owner, 10% of all dividends or distributions of Community Cable TV—the cable television system serving Las Vegas and surrounding areas—and to ultimately transfer 10% ownership in the system and provide an option to purchase another 35% ownership in the system. That cable TV portion of the deal was reportedly worth $20 million (Stein, 1989). The agreement also included a provision for switching the publication cycle of the newspapers, moving the *Sun* to the evening and the *Review-Journal* to the morning.

Although it included the sweetener of cable television ownership, the JOA application raised little opposition. Its approval without hearing was recommended by the Antitrust Division, and the Attorney General approved the application.

The developments in these cases have focused on three major issues: (a) When does a newspaper meet the "failing newspaper" criteria? (b) Can the factors causing failure become an issue? (c) Are there limits to the ability of the Attorney General to approve an application? A review of how those issues have been handled across the applications provides a clear view of the import attached to various factors in making the determinations.

TESTS OF WHETHER A NEWSPAPER IS FAILING

In examining the eight applications and decisions by the Attorney General, one can see that a variety of indicators have been used to determine whether a newspaper meets the "failing newspaper" criteria. From the legislative hearings and subsequent applications, however, three main tests of failure emerge: (a) significant market share disparities, (b) presence of the circulation spiral, and (c) financial losses.

Market Share Disparity

The first test of failure considers whether significant disparities exist between the market shares of competing newspapers for circulation and advertising. This is important because as market share declines, the secondary newspaper comes increasingly close to failure.

Two indicators are used to determine market shares of applicants and the degree to which disparities exist: (a) the average paid circulation achieved, and (b) advertising sales, evidenced by lineage or revenue.

These two indicators are important because there is an interaction between circulation share and advertising share of newspapers. A disproportionate share of advertising is given to the newspaper with the larger circulation. When a newspaper exceeds the 50% circulation level, its share of advertising is disproportionately high. For example, a newspaper with a 60% share of circulation will generally have an advertising share of approximately 75%. When the circulation share is low, for example, 40%, the advertising share will generally be approximately 25% (Picard, 1988d, pp. 60–61).

Evidence indicates that a serious problem develops for the smaller newspaper when a 55 to 45% circulation share split occurs, a critical problem exists when a 60 to 40% circulation market share develops, and failure occurs at about a 65 to 35% share split (Picard, 1987, p. 76).

Advertising shares, measured by the percentage of revenues or lineage, are equally important. An industry rule of thumb states that when the split between two newspapers exceeds approximately 55 to 45%, the disparity begins to become serious. In situations where the split is more than 60 to 40%, it becomes critical. Thus the significance of the 55 to 45 and 60 to 40 share split applies to both advertising and circulation.

The "Circulation Spiral"

The second, and most significant, test put forth in legislative discussion considers whether a "circulation spiral" exists. This phenomenon occurs when declining circulation results in declining advertising sales, affecting the ability of the newspaper to keep editorial quality high and provide desired advertising information to readers. As a result, continuing losses in circulation occur, with subsequent losses of more advertising, until the newspaper spirals to its death (Furhoff, 1973; Gustafsson, 1978). The danger of the downward spiral of circulation was recognized during efforts to enact the NPA and has since been cited in every application and hearing for a JOA since its passage (Inouye, 1970; Rosse, 1981; Morton, 1981).

This problem is compounded because the newspaper with the largest circulation in a given market is able to increase circulation and advertising revenues at the expense of the smaller newspaper and use those revenues to force the smaller newspaper into less advantageous marketing situations (Furhoff, 1973; Picard, 1988b). The leading newspaper can use the additional revenue to heighten editorial, advertising, production, and delivery quality to a level that the competitor cannot meet or that will bankrupt the secondary newspaper if it attempts to maintain such quality. As a result, the smaller newspaper's economic difficulties are increased and it is pushed into the downward circulation spiral that leads to increasing problems in selling advertising space (Engwall, 1981; Gustafsson, 1978).

The two indicators of the circulation spiral are the same as those used to measure market share disparities: (a) the average paid circulation, and (b) advertising sales measured in lineage or revenue. When reviewed over time—five or ten years for example—these indicators can establish whether such a spiral has developed.

Financial Losses

The third major test to determine whether a newspaper is failing is the existence of financial losses. In this case, the relevant measure is real operating losses that are unlikely to be reversed.

The standard imposed in passing this test is that the management of the failing newspaper has made reasonable and substantial efforts to halt losses and that there is no significant prospect that the losses can be reversed in the future. This standard has been established in NPA case law as meaning that a failing newspaper is "suffering losses which more than likely cannot be reversed" (Committee for an Independent *Post-Intelligencer*, 1983, 704 F.2d at 478; *Michigan Citizens*, 1989, 868 F.2d at 1292).

Newspapers filing applications to form JOAs since passage of the NPA have passed the three primary tests of failure to varying degrees.

Market Share Disparities Shown

The sizes of the gaps between circulation and advertising shares of the two competing newspapers in each of the eight markets prior to establishment of JOAs are unique to each situation, but the newspapers' performances conform to the anticipated economic patterns of disparity (Figure 3.2).

In terms of circulation share, the *Anchorage News* was clearly at a disadvantage with only 26.9% of total circulation in its market in 1973, compared with 73.1% share for the *Anchorage Times*.

In Chattanooga, the *News-Free Press* garnered 53.5% of total circulation, 54.3% of metro area circulation, and 53.7% of city zone circulation in 1979. In contrast, the *Times* had a total circulation of only 46.5%, with 45.7% of the metro area circulation and 46.8% of city zone circulation.

The Cincinnati circulation share split was much tighter. In 1979, for example, the *Enquirer* accounted for 50.7% of total circulation, 48.6% of metro area circulation, and 49.5% of city zone circulation. The competing *Post* garnered 49.3% of total circulation, 51.4% of metro circulation, and 50.5% of city zone circulation.

54 JOINT OPERATING AGREEMENTS

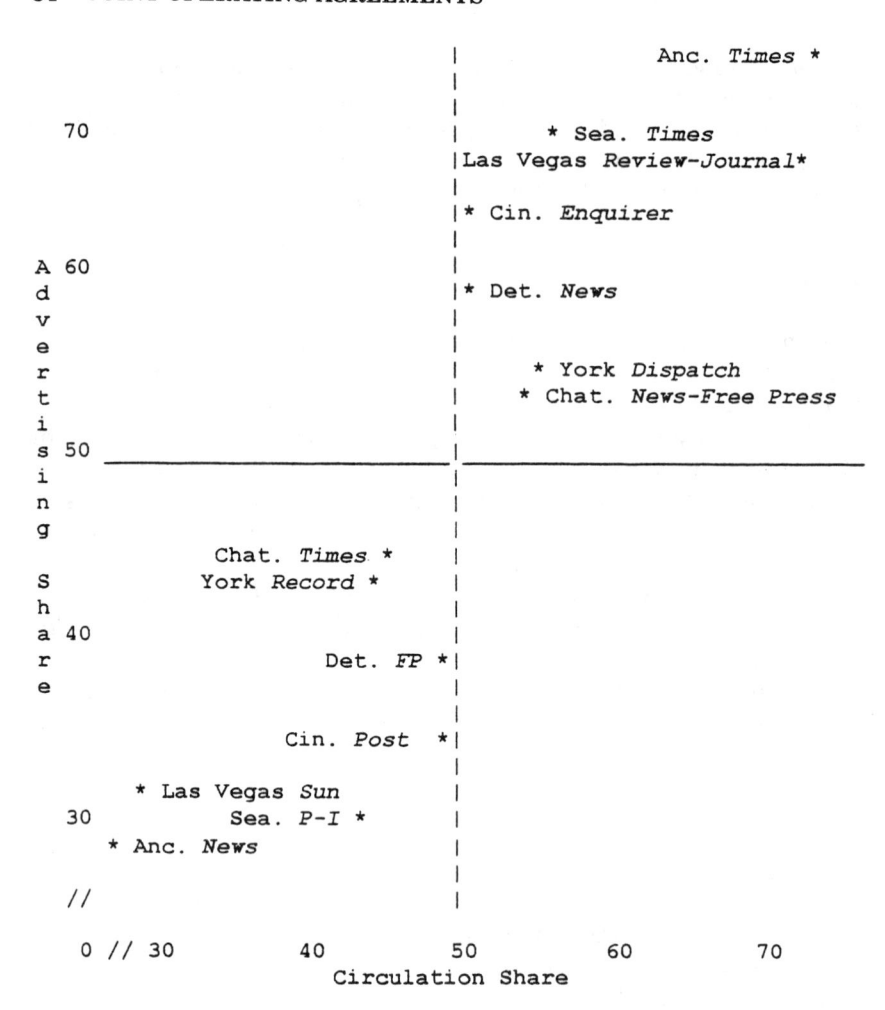

```
                                    |              Anc. Times *
                                    |
                                    |
         70                         |      * Sea. Times
                                    |Las Vegas Review-Journal*
                                    |
                                    |* Cin. Enquirer
                                    |
A        60                         |
d                                   |* Det. News
v                                   |
e                                   |
r                                   |      * York Dispatch
t                                   |      * Chat. News-Free Press
i                                   |
s        50 _____ |_____
i                                   |
n                                   |
g                                   |
                  Chat. Times *     |
S                 York Record *     |
h                                   |
a        40                         |
r                       Det. FP *   |
e                                   |
                                    |
                      Cin. Post   * |
                                    |
              * Las Vegas Sun       |
         30              Sea. P-I * |
                * Anc. News         |
                                    |
         //                         |
            0 // 30       40       50       60       70
                         Circulation Share
```

Figure 3.2. Disparity Between Advertising and Circulation Shares in Newspapers Entering JOAs Since 1970

The Detroit circulation share split was also tight when that city's papers applied for a JOA in 1985. The *Free Press* held 49.6% of the total circulation, 45% of the primary marketing area circulation, and 46% of the city and retail trading zone circulation. The competing *News* garnered 51.4% of the total circulation, with 55% of the circulation in the primary marketing area and 54% of the circulation in the city and retail trading zones.

A much greater circulation disparity was evident in Las Vegas, where the *Review-Journal* garnered 70.6% of total daily circulation and the *Sun* provided only 29.4% of daily circulation.

Analysis of market share disparity cannot be comparably made in the Manteca case because the application involved a daily and a weekly newspaper whose product markets, although similar, were not directly substitutable. Thus an indication of market share disparities between the two newspapers would not be similar to those of the other applications.

In 1980, the Seattle *Post-Intelligencer* held 43.3% of total circulation, 37.1% of the metro area circulation, and 37.2% of city zone circulation. By comparison, the *Times* accounted for 56.7% of total circulation, 62.9% of metro area circulation and 62.8% of city zone circulation.

In York, the *Record* held 44.8% of the total daily circulation and 44.3% in the combined city and retail trading zone. This compared to a 55.2% total circulation share and a 55.7% share for the combined city and retail trading zone for the *Dispatch*.

Similar discrepancies existed in terms of advertising shares for the newspapers. In Anchorage, the *Times* enjoyed a 3-to-1 advantage over the *News* in 1973, receiving approximately 75% of the advertising shares. The *Chattanooga Times* accounted for 45.1% of the shares in that city in 1979, compared to 54.9% for the *News-Free Press*. In Cincinnati in 1976, the *Enquirer* garnered a 65.5% share of advertising, while the *Post* acquired only 34.5%. The Detroit ad shares in 1985 also revealed a wide split. The *News* was responsible for 61.6% of the share, and the *Free Press* accounted for 38.4%.

The Las Vegas *Review-Journal* dominated the *Sun* in the advertising market, accounting for 70.4% of the column inches published, with the *Sun* attracting 29.6%. Although this gives an indication of the disparity between the two, the measure is not directly comparable to that given for newspapers in other JOA applications because comparisons for those newspapers are made on the basis of advertising revenue. Such a comparison is not possible in the Las Vegas case because the *Review-Journal* asked the Attorney General not to release its financial information. The advertising revenue and share data were removed from public documents in the case. The Las Vegas application is the only one in which advertising revenue figures were not available.

As with the case of circulation market share, the disparity in advertising shares for the weekly and daily newspapers applying for a JOA in Manteca are not applicable because of differences in their advertising product markets.

In Seattle in 1980, the *Post-Intelligencer* held only 29.5% of the advertising share compared to 70.5% for the *Times*. The market shares in York, PA, for the applicants in 1983 were 44.3% of inches published and 45% of revenues for the *Record*, compared to 55.7% of inches published and 55% of revenues for the *Dispatch*.

The Circulation Spiral

The second test is the presence of the downward "circulation spiral," that is, losses in circulation and advertising that increase over time. Of the eight newspapers seeking JOAs, only five provided evidence of the existence of the downward circulation spiral.

In Anchorage, the *News'* circulation declined from 16,551 in 1965 to 15,079 in 1973. During the same period, the circulation of the rival *Times* rose from 28,988 to 41,069. The advertising situation of the *News* paralleled its declining circulation situation, a problem that was compounded because the *Times* was able to sell advertising at half the milline rate of the *News*.

In the case of the *Chattanooga Times*, the spiral was evident in a decrease in circulation from 58,907 in 1975 to 51,072 in 1979 and in the *Times'* decreasing share of ad revenue from 50% in 1976 to 45.1% in 1979.

In Cincinnati, the *Post* experienced a decrease in circulation from 252,000 in 1964 to 181,842 in 1979 and a decrease in advertising revenue share from 36.1% in 1975 to approximately 15% in 1977.

The *Detroit Free Press* experienced an increase in circulation from 605,156 in 1980 to 644,778 in 1985. Its ad revenue share increased from 38.2% in 1981 to 38.4% in 1985.

The *Las Vegas Sun's* circulation had risen from 47,637 in September 1979 to 53,948 when it applied for its JOA. The circulation had declined somewhat after peaking in the mid-1980s. Despite the increase in circulation itself during the 1980s, the circulation share of the *Sun* had been declining rather steadily as it failed to keep up with the growth of the *Review-Journal*. In 1979, its circulation share amounted to 38% of daily circulation but that figure had declined to about 30% when the JOA application was filed. The decline can be seen in the amount of column inches published. In 1984, the *Sun* published about 2 million column inches of advertising, but by 1988 that figure had declined to 1.3 million column inches.

During the decade-long competition between the newspapers in Manteca, the *News* increased its circulation markedly from 0 to 5,000 for its paid edition and from 0 to 18,000 for its free circulation edition. Circulation grew continuously and thus the newspaper provided no evidence of a downward circulation spiral. Likewise, circulation and advertising trends were both upwards for the *Record* in York, Pa., so the downward circulation spiral did not exist there.

The *Seattle Post-Intelligencer* experienced a decrease in circulation from 213,171 in 1961 to 182,475 in 1981. Its ad revenue share decreased from 33.4% in 1976 to 29.5% in 1980.

Financial Losses

The third indicator of failure is financial losses, measured in dollars or as a portion of revenue. In Anchorage, for example, losses for the *News* averaged 49% of revenues from 1966-1974, and averaged $500,000 annually from 1969 to 1974.

In Chattanooga, losses for the *Times* rose significantly in the four years prior to its application for a JOA. Losses of $377,000 in 1976 grew to $1.2 million in 1979. Losses for the *Cincinnati Post* were 4.5% of revenues in 1977. The *Detroit Free Press* encountered losses of 5.2% of revenues in 1985. Owners of the *Las Vegas Sun* experienced financial losses for seven years prior to the JOA application, losing $3.6 million in 1988 alone, and $13 million between 1981 and 1988.

Between 1977 and 1988 the *News* in Manteca, experienced losses of between $10 and $12 million, with up to $6.3 million involving litigation costs and payments to the *Bulletin* in an antitrust suit for predatory advertising pricing. Beyond those costs, the *News* experienced losses of about $500,000 annually, which may be more attributable to startup costs and investments than operating losses.

The *Record* in York experienced an operating loss of 1.6% of its revenues in 1988 and about $4 million between 1978 and 1988. The *Seattle Post-Intelligencer* lost 3.9% of revenues in 1980, just prior to its application for a JOA.

The three tests of failure provide five indicators by which to judge whether failure exists. The eight newspapers that have sought JOAs have had different patterns of indicators of failure, as revealed in Table 3.1.

Of the newspapers granted JOAs, all passed at least four of the tests of failure, with the *Anchorage News* and *Seattle Post-Intelligencer* scoring perfect 5s. Only the *Detroit Free Press* did *not* pass the majority of the five tests, for it provides only two of the five indicators of failure. It showed no evidence of the downward circulation spiral.

CAN FACTORS CAUSING FAILURE BE AN ISSUE?

The question of the extent to which the above tests indicate failure has been raised in several applications. Both administrative law and court rulings have recognized that how financial losses occurred and the effects of management practices and decisions may be relevant to the determination of whether an applicant actually meets the failing newspaper criteria.

The desire to ensure that financial losses cited by the newspaper are

58 JOINT OPERATING AGREEMENTS

Table 3.1. Indicators of Failure in Newspapers Seeking JOA Approvals

City	Downward Spiral Circ.	Downward Spiral Adv.	Disparity Circ.	Disparity Adv.	Financial Loss	Total Yes
Anchorage	Y	Y	Y-C	Y-C	Y	5
Chattanooga	Y	Y	N	Y-S	Y	4
Cincinnati	Y	Y	N	Y-C	Y	4
Detroit	N	N	N	Y-C	Y	2
Las Vegas	Y	Y	Y-C	Y-C	Y	5
Manteca	N	N	N.A.	N.A.	Y*	1
Seattle	Y	Y	Y-S	Y-C	Y	5
York	N	N	Y-S	Y-S	Y	3
Total Yes	5	5	4	7	8	

Legend:
N = No
Y = Yes
Y-C = Yes, Critical Disparity (see text)
Y-S = Yes, Serious Disparity (see text)
N.A. = Not Available
*These losses are disputed due to payments for antitrust litigation.

real and irreversible emerged clearly in 1979 with the decision of the administrative law judge in the application for the Cincinnati JOA. In that decision, the judge ruled that overcharges from news, feature, and advertising services provided by the E. W. Scripps Company had to be eliminated from the accounts before a determination was made on whether the *Cincinnati Post* was a failing newspaper (Moore, 1979, p. 56). In doing so, he removed some payments to the *Post*'s parent company from expenses, recognizing that these should not be considered normal operating expenses and setting a precedent for disputing the validity of expenses cited as factors in losses.

The ability of applicants to argue that losses are irreversible despite their cause was also tempered by the Ninth Circuit Court of Appeals in its opinion on the Seattle application. The court stated that newspapers are to be prevented "from allowing or encouraging financial difficulties in the hopes of reaping long-term financial gains through a JOA" (Committee for an Independent *Post-Intelligencer*, 1983, 704 F.2d at 478). This ruling, then, specifically provided that the causes of losses were relevant issues for consideration in applications.

The decisions made by management could be considered, the court said, but it also stated that the NPA was not strict in its requirements. "Generally...the burden [of proving failure] only entails a showing of (1) the economic fact of probable failure (downward spiral, irreversible losses), and (2) reasonable management practices," the court said (Committee for an Independent *Post-Intelligencer*, 1983, 704 F.2d at 478).

In the hearings on the Detroit application, questions over the reasonableness of the *Free Press* decision to engage in "Operation

Tiger," a campaign to dominate the *News*, and whether its associated costs could be legitimately counted as losses to prove the *Free Press* a failing newspaper emerged (Kwoka, 1988; Needelman, 1987, p. 66). Opponents argued that the campaign was a make-or-break plan for the newspaper and that it would either become the dominant Detroit newspaper or lose sufficient money to make the newspaper eligible for a JOA as a failing newspaper.

The Antitrust Division and the administrative law judge both concluded that the decisions of the *Free Press*' management were unreasonable and contributed to its losses and that the newspaper did not meet the failing newspaper criteria. Their conclusions and recommendations, however, were ignored by the Attorney General who chose to grant approval.

In litigation following that decision, opponents of the Detroit decision raised another significant factor in the case. In court arguments, particularly during oral hearings before the Supreme Court, the role that predatory pricing of advertising and circulation in Detroit may have played in creating financial losses and other indicators of failure was raised significantly.

Opponents to the Attorney General's decision argued that if anticompetitive acts resulted in a newspaper meeting the failing newspaper criteria, their effect should be excluded from consideration. The benefits of a JOA under the NPA should not be the result of illegal acts, they contended. Instead, the failing newspaper or the government should seek antitrust enforcement and damages for the actions.

A few judges and justices voiced some apparent support for the predatory pricing argument at both the Court of Appeals and Supreme Court levels. This predation argument had been raised in public comments submitted to the Department of Justice and in the research literature (Busterna, 1986, 1988a, 1988b, 1988c, 1989a, 1989b). However, the JOA opponents' legal counsel waited until the appeals process to raise this issue so that it technically could not be considered by the appeals courts. Nevertheless, this new consideration of the cause of failure raises another avenue of inquiry for disputing some evidences of failure in future cases.

Is the Attorney General's Approval Power Limited?

The ability of the Attorney General to make decisions about applications, and the criteria that he must employ, has also been raised in the appeals of decisions made by applicants.

The most sweeping decision came in the Detroit case, which recognized that the Attorney General's power over procedures and criteria is nearly unlimited by the NPA. The Court of Appeals'

60 JOINT OPERATING AGREEMENTS

decision noted that the Attorney General is not "legally obliged to conform his judgment to that of a statutorially-required ALJ [administrative law judge]" but that his actions must only be reasonable. The court noted that Congress had "delegated to the Attorney General . . . the delicate and troubling responsibility of putting content into the ambiguous phrase 'probable danger of financial failure.' We cannot therefore say that his interpretation of the phrase as applied to this case, with all of its obvious policy implications, was unreasonable" (Michigan Citizens for an Independent Press v. Thornburgh, 1989).

Thus, it appears that as long as the Attorney General acts with a rationale that does not contradict the intention of the NPA to provide newspapers protections from antitrust enforcement if they cease competition and join operations, and one newspaper may reasonably be argued to be in danger of failure, his actions will be permitted even if his view contradicts those of other parties empowered to investigate the claim.

Recommendations and Decisions by the Attorney General

The power of the U.S. Attorney General to make decisions then begs the question of the extent to which the Attorney General and others who make determinations agree.

Despite the weak tests of failure and the general preference toward JOAs built into the NPA, the Antitrust Division has opposed three of the eight applications. Table 3.2 reports the recommendations of the Antitrust Division on each application.

The Attorney General has twice chosen not to follow the negative recommendations placed before him by his Antitrust Division, in the Detroit and Seattle cases (Table 3.3), and only once—in the Manteca application—has he ordered a hearing when the division recom-

Table 3.2. Recommendations on Applications by the Antitrust Division

City	Approval Warranted	Nonapproval Warranted	Hold Hearing	Hearing Unnecessary
Anchorage	X			X
Chattanooga	X*			X
Cincinnati			X	
Detroit		X	X	
Las Vegas	X			X
Manteca		X		X
Seattle		X	X	
York	X			X

*After recommending nonapproval because of early start of joint operations.

Table 3.3. Actions by the Attorney General on Approval and Nonapproval Recommendations

City	Followed Recommendation of Antitrust Division	Followed Recommedation of Admin. Law Judge
Anchorage	Yes	Not applicable No hearings held
Chattanooga	Yes	Not applicable No hearings held
Cincinnati		Yes
Detroit	No	No
Las Vegas	Yes	Not applicable No hearings held
Manteca	No*	
Seattle	No	Yes
York	Yes	Not applicable No hearings held

*No to recommendation that hearings not be held.

mended otherwise. In all cases in which the division recommended that hearings be held to determine fact, the Attorney General has ordered them. The Attorney General has only once—in the Detroit case—disregarded the recommendation of the administrative law judge after hearing.

The wide latitude of the Attorney General to make decisions on the application, regardless of hearing record or evidence that leads to a negative decision by the Department of Justice is a result of the breadth of the NPA. The NPA does not provide that applications require strict administrative law procedures, nor does it directly stipulate which criteria shall be used, and what weight given to each, by the Attorney General in deciding that an approval is warranted. The ability of the Attorney General to make a decision based on his own judgment or expediency rather than the findings of the administrative law judge and Antitrust Division is problematic because it dilutes the process of serious consideration of the appropriateness of an application for the antitrust exemption.

If one reviews the chronology of applications it is clear that recent decisions have placed relatively less emphasis on the advertising and circulation disparities and the circulation spiral tests of failure and greater emphasis on financial losses alone.

However, the tests themselves are weak because they are merely indicators of strength or lack of strength used in conjunction with a statute designed to ease the way to JOAs. The fact that the NPA provides a less stringent standard of evidence of failure than the "failing company" antitrust test applied to other industries allows the Attorney General far greater ability to grant JOA applications, and makes it almost impossible to halt a proposed JOA.

The weakness of the tests applied is evidenced in the Antitrust Division's analysis of the York application:

> This is a close case. From a financial standpoint the *Record* is not compelled instantly to shut its door; nor do advertising and circulation trends show that the *Record* has already entered the fatal downward spiral of contracting revenues and readership. Nevertheless, Congress' test of "probable danger" stops short of requiring that a newspaper's failure be virtually imminent or totally certain. Parsing the statute strictly but fairly, a newspaper may qualify under Congress' test where the newspaper shows that financial failure in the reasonably near future is highly probable and that all reasonable efforts to rescue the newspaper have been exhausted. (Boudin, 1989, pp. 52–53)

Given the ambiguities attached to such a determination and its preference toward approval, it appears highly unlikely that any JOA application between competing daily newspapers will be denied in the near future.

4
Legislative Initiatives Regarding The NPA

Efforts to amend the Newspaper Preservation Act have been undertaken by supporters and opponents of joint operating agreements, especially during the mid- and late 1980s. In that time, two amendments have been proposed and considered, and Congress has held oversight hearings on the NPA. A bill to repeal the NPA altogether was introduced in the House of Representatives during the 101st Congress and is expected to be revived shortly.

Initial efforts to modify the NPA were made in the mid-1980s by publishers of JOA newspapers who were seeking specific authorization and exemptions to expand their publishing activities. The publishers were unsuccessful in their efforts, and their activities helped coalesce opponents of JOAs and the NPA, leading to significant public criticism of the NPA and to the subsequent effort to repeal it.

S. 2314

The first attempt to modify the NPA occurred in the spring of 1986 when Senators Orrin Hatch (R-UT), Jake Garn (R-UT), and Daniel Inouye (D-HI) introduced a measure into the Senate to revise the NPA. This proposed revision would change the definition of a newspaper, allow JOA newspapers to broaden their permitted publishing activities, and allow JOA newspapers to become involved in electronic information delivery. The proposal, S. 2314 (Figure 4.1), was referred to the Committee on the Judiciary, which held hearings on June 10, 1986.

Figure 4.1. S. 2314 as Introduced

A BILL

To amend the Newspaper Preservation Act.

Be it enacted by the Senate and House of Representatives of the United States of America in Congress assembled, That section 3(4) of the Newspaper Preservation Act (15 U. S. C. 1802(4)), is amended by—

(i) striking out "on newsprint paper which is published"; and

(ii) striking out "and in which" and inserting in lieu thereof "and delivered in whole or in part to readers and in which whole publication."

Sec. 2. Section 4(c) of the Newspaper Preservation Act (15 U. S. C. 1803(c)), is amended by—

(1) striking out "the Act" in the first sentence and inserting in lieu thereof "this Act"; and

(2) inserting between the first and second sentences the following: "Nor shall anything in this Act be construed to make unlawful under any antitrust law any activity undertaken by a party to a joint newspaper operating agreement in connection with a newspaper publication that could be engaged in lawfully if such person were not a party to such an arrangement."

The simplicity of the bill—only 21 lines and less than 160 words in length—belied its intended effects, much like the simplicity of the original bill proposing the NPA in the 1960s.

Senator Hatch indicated that he introduced the bill at the request of the *Tribune* and *Deseret News*, the Salt Lake City JOA newspapers that dominate the senator's home state (Roper, 1986). How and why the other two senators chose to join the reconsideration of the NPA is unclear, but the fact that they represent two states where the four leading newspapers operate JOAs is undoubtedly germane. The proposed amendment came on the heels of litigation in Arizona in which a semiweekly newspaper, the *Green Valley News*, challenged the ability of the Tucson *Star* and *Citizen* JOA to operate a free circulation total market coverage "shopper" in the market in which the smaller newspaper operated (Wick v. Tucson Newspapers, 1984).

The measure was introduced after the U.S. District Court in Tucson ruled that operation of the shopper by the JOA newspapers violated the NPA and the U.S. Supreme Court ruling that earlier upheld the terms of the statute. The District Court ordered the JOA newspapers to halt publication of the total market coverage shopper and indicated that the Tucson newspapers could be sued for antitrust violations because their shopper activities were not exempted from antitrust laws by the NPA.

The proposed amendments and statements supporting the bill by its sponsors never specifically mentioned the Arizona case. When the hearings on the bill were held, Judiciary Committee Chair Strom Thurmond (R-SC) was absent and Senator Hatch acted as chair of the hearing.

In his opening statement, Senator Hatch justified S. 2314 by asserting that "JOAs have served their purpose well." However, he argued that since the passage of the NPA, "the newspaper publishing business has changed markedly. This necessitates an updating of the Newspaper Preservation Act" (Hearings on S. 2314, 1987, p. 1).

Hatch's views were echoed by Senator Inouye, who had been a sponsor of the NPA when it was originally considered by Congress. Inouye argued that the proposed amendment was necessary to allow newspapers to print on slick paper rather than newsprint and to enter the electronic publishing field.

Support for the proposal at the hearings was provided in testimony and statements submitted by representatives of JOA newspapers in Charleston, WV; Salt Lake City, UT; San Francisco, CA; Shreveport, LA; and Tulsa, OK. Following the lead of the bill's sponsors, the JOA supporters outlined the benefits of the NPA and argued that the bill was needed to allow JOA newspapers to make changes in response to contemporary developments. Like the bill's sponsors, the supporters specifically avoided reference to the Arizona case, and made only passing references to the desire of newspapers to produce total market coverage newspapers.

The proponents characterized the amendment as providing technical revisions that merely updated the NPA to make it more contemporary. However, the proposal drew heavy criticism and opposition from publishers of suburban daily and weekly newspapers. They believed that the revisions would allow JOA newspapers to enter into direct competition with them and give the JOA newspapers the unfair economic advantage of using the antitrust exemption to allow cost savings in their competition with non-JOA newspapers.

The industry group that led the opponents, Suburban Newspapers of America, passed a resolution at its 1986 annual meeting calling the amendment "unnecessary" and "bad public policy," arguing that the result of its passage "would be to silence the editorial voice of the suburban newspaper industry." Richard Aginian, a past president of this trade association, argued that Congress had explicitly excluded slick paper, magazines, shoppers, and advertising sheets from the antitrust exemption of the NPA and that revising the act to include them would allow JOA newspapers to use their size, economic strength, and antitrust exemption to harm smaller non-JOA newspapers.

John Frank, an attorney who represented the owner of the weekly newspaper that challenged the Tucson JOA newspapers, told the Judiciary Committee that if JOA newspapers were allowed to circulate free shoppers, "the practical effect will be to pull the advertisers out of the existing suburban papers and move them over to the free shoppers" (Frank, 1986).

The American Newspaper Publishers Association, the primary lobbying organization for the industry, did not take a stand or testify at the hearings, reflecting division among its members and the strong opposition of small daily newspapers whose managers felt they might be hurt by the measure. The National Newspaper Association, which represents smaller newspapers, opposed the measure following a policy set by its board in June, 1986 to vigorously oppose any proposals that might expand the NPA.

Robert G. Picard, one of the authors of this book, told the committee that changes were not necessary for the survival of any JOA newspaper, that the proposed changes treated all JOA newspaper markets as similar despite differences in size and other economic characteristics, and that the changes would provide unusual economies of scale for the JOA production of total market coverage shoppers. These economies, he stated, would harm suburban dailies and weeklies in some markets (Picard, 1986a).

Opposition also came from the Department of Justice, which argued that ancillary operations, such as total market coverage newspapers and electronic publication, were not essential portions of operations necessary for the survival of a JOA (Hearings on S. 2314, pp. 213-217). Assistant Attorney General John Bolton said that the proposed amendment did little to clarify the law, and "it expands the scope of activities in some ways that have not been justified on the current record" (Hearings on S. 2314, p. 219).

The strong opposition to the measure voiced at the hearing was ignored by the committee, which reported the bill favorably to the full Senate and recommended its passage. The decision was not surprising to opponents of the measure because many believed that the hearing had been orchestrated by Senator Hatch. For example, amendment supporters had been supplied opponents' prepared testimony so that they could attempt to refute it in their own testimony, whereas opponents were not given a similar opportunity.

Membership of the committee also included eight senators from states with JOA newspapers directly affected by the proposed amendment. These senators included Hatch, Howell Heflin (D-AL), Howard Metzenbaum (D-OH), and Dennis DeConcini (D-AZ). Although some of the senators were later to question the wisdom of the proposal, most opponents felt that the committee's intent was clearly to promote the interests of JOA publishers.

Figure 4.2. S. 2314 as Reported From Committee

A BILL

To amend the Newspaper Preservation Act.

Be it enacted by the Senate and House of Representatives of the United States of America in Congress assembled, That (a) section 3(2) of the Newspaper Preservation Act (Public Law 91-353; 15 U. S. C. 1802(2)) is amended by inserting after "distribution" the first time it appears the following: "of all or part of such newspaper publications."

(b) Section 4(b) of such Act (15 U. S. C. 1803(b)) is amended by striking out the first sentence and inserting in lieu thereof the following: "It shall not be unlawful for any person to enter into, perform, or enforce a joint operating agreement not already in effect, if the prior written consent of the Attorney General has been obtained."

(c) Section 4 of such Act (*15 U. S. C. 1803) is amended by adding at the end thereof the following new subsection:

"(d) In any action under any antitrust law challenging joint conduct between the parties to a joint newspaper operating arrangement that has received the limited antitrust exemption provided by subsection (a) or (b) of this section, joint conduct between the parties that is not exempt as part of such arrangement but that is reasonably ancillary to the business of publishing the newspaper publications involved in the arrangement shall not be deemed illegal per se. Such joint conduct shall be judged on the basis of its reasonableness, taking into account all relevant factors affecting competition in properly defined relevant markets."

After the hearing, the committee dropped the part of the amendment that would have expanded the NPA's definition of a newspaper beyond just those publications printed on newsprint. However, the amended version maintained the intention to allow newspapers to use their JOA operations to produce total market coverage newspapers and shoppers as subsidiary publications, to alter the NPA so it would indicate that such subsidiary publications were not unlawful, and to require courts to use the antitrust rule of reason approach when adjudicating disputes involving JOA newspapers' subsidiary publications, rather than the easier to prove *per se* rule normally used in restraint of trade cases (Figure 4.2).

Senators Metzenbaum and DeConcini separated themselves from the committee report. Metzenbaum noted that the committee itself carried out "only limited debate" on the bill and that it had agreed to report the bill without recommendation, a decision that had become a recommendation for passage when Senator Thurmond wrote the report. The Ohio senator called for a broad review of the NPA and not "piecemeal" legislation, saying that criticisms of the NPA—such as the need to search for alternative buyers before approval of a JOA and the need to refine the definition of a failing newspaper—had merit (Senate Report 539, 1986, pp. 20–21).

Senator DeConcini completely rejected the report, stating that the amendment went well beyond the intent of the legislators who had debated the original NPA in the 1960s and that "the bill now before us turns the Newspaper Preservation Act on its head" (Senate Report 539, 1986, p. 23). The Arizona senator took the side of smaller newspapers, arguing that approval of the measure would provide JOA newspapers a means of destroying the financial support of the smaller editorial voices.

Despite the efforts of the supporters of the measure, loud opposition by JOA detractors and concerns such as those expressed by Metzenbaum and DeConcini kept S. 2314 from gaining momentum. The bill never received another hearing in the Senate and died when the second session of the 99th Congress ended.

However, opponents of the measure used the bill to create a strong, antiamendment coalition aimed at defeating any measure that might provide JOA newspapers additional strength should they choose to directly compete with non-JOA newspapers. The coalition included not only the Suburban Newspapers of America, but also the National Newspaper Association, the California Newspaper Publishers Association, the Utah Press Association, and scores of publishers concerned about the power of the large publishers covered by the NPA.

These groups expressed concern that Senator Hatch would reintroduce the bill in the 100th Congress, a concern that was not allayed because JOA publishers were still promoting the measure and because the senator's staff would not indicate his intention toward the measure (Stein, 1987).

In 1988, growing concern over the issue led the board of directors of the National Newspapers Association to commission a major review and analysis of the NPA by its general counsel. The study dismissed the possibility of seeking repeal of the NPA or Justice Department review of JOA abuses, but suggested that the group begin participating in proceedings of future applications for JOA approval and that it continue its opposition to expansion of the NPA (Brinkman, 1988).

AMENDMENT 2509 TO S. 430

The publishers' concern that another effort would be made to provide JOA newspapers antitrust protection for total market coverage newspapers was not unfounded. In 1988, during the 100th Congress, Senator Inouye led another attempt to modify the NPA. The continuing support for the JOA publishers on the part of senators from states with JOA newspapers once again revealed that party lines and political ideology are not important factors when it comes to the NPA. In the 99th Congress, efforts to help JOA publishers were led by Senator Hatch and the Republican majority. In the 100th Congress, efforts to help JOA publishers were led by Senator Inouye and the new Democratic majority.

However, this time no bill was introduced. Instead, the effort was made in the form of a Senate amendment, 2509 (Figure 4.3), which was added to S. 430, a bill updating and codifying antitrust law. The amendment was cosponsored, to the surprise of many, by Howard Metzenbaum, author of S. 430. The amendment set off a storm of opposition from small newspapers (Milligan, 1988).

The amendment's primary section was intended to expand the NPA to ensure that subsidiary operations by JOA newspapers, such as total market coverage publications, were not precluded by the NPA. The measure stipulated that "joint conduct between the parties that is not exempt as a part of such arrangement but that is reasonably ancillary to the business of publishing the newspaper publications involved in the arrangement shall not be deemed illegal per se." The measure then went on to define the test of whether such acts should be permitted, saying ancillary joint conduct should be "judged on the

Figure 4.3. Senate Amendment 2509 to S. 430

At the end of the pending matter add the following:
(a) Section 3(2) of the Newspaper Preservation Act (Public Law 91-353; 15 U. S. C. 1803(6)) is amended by inserting after "distribution" the first time it appears the following: "of all or part of such newspaper publications."
(b) Section 3(4) of such Act (15 U. S. C. 1803(4)) is amended by inserting after "produced" the following: "in whole or in part."
(c) Section 4 of such Act (15 U. S. C. 1803(6)) is amended by striking out the first sentence and inserting in lieu thereof the following: "It shall not be unlawful for any person to enter into, perform, or enforce a joint operating agreement not already in effect, if the prior written consent of the Attorney General has been obtained."
(d) Section 4 of such Act (*15 U. S. C. 1803(6)) is amended by adding at the end thereof the following new subsection:
"(d) In any action under any antitrust law challenging joint conduct between the parties to a joint newspaper operating arrangement that has received the limited antitrust exemption provided by subsection (a) or (b) of this section, joint conduct between the parties that is not exempt as part of such arrangement but that is reasonably ancillary to the business of publishing the newspaper publications involved in the arrangement shall not be deemed illegal per se. Such joint conduct shall be judged on the basis of its reasonableness, taking into account all relevant factors affecting competition in properly defined relevant markets."

basis of its reasonableness, taking into account all relevant factors affecting competition in properly defined relevant markets" (*Congressional Record-Senate*, 1988, S8820–8821).

The proposed amendment was a near clone of the bill reported favorably by the Judiciary Committee in the previous session of Congress. Its sudden appearance with the support of Metzenbaum, who had earlier separated himself from the bill and called for full hearings on the NPA, shocked many opponents. However, the continuing support of the proposal by Senator Inouye was expected.

Speaking in support of the amendment, Senator Inouye told of the efforts he and Senator Hatch had made in the 99th Congress, giving the impression that little opposition had existed to S. 2314: "The Judiciary Committee held hearings, and favorably reported the bill, recommending its passage" (*Congressional Record-Senate*, 1988, S. 8775). His view bolstered that of Metzenbaum, who had earlier told the Senate that Senate Republicans, who had been the majority party in the 99th Congress, had "voted for a similar amendment in the . . . Judiciary Committee, and I guess they would find it acceptable at this point" (*Congressional Record-Senate*, 1988, S8774).

The tactic used by Inouye and Metzenbaum was seen as an effort to bypass the Congressional committee system and overcome opposition that had developed when S. 2314 was considered. Senator Metzenbaum's staff seemed genuinely surprised by the controversy that ensued and indicated that he had introduced and cosponsored the amendment at the request of Senator Inouye. As opposition grew and his office was bombarded with protests, Metzenbaum withdrew the amendment and dropped his cosponsorship, effectively killing the amendment.

Opponents of the measure were pleased with the result, but charged that JOA supporters in the Senate were using influence and a legislative back door to achieve their goals. Bruce Brugmann, publisher of the weekly *San Francisco Bay Guardian*, who had opposed the NPA when it was first proposed in the 1960s, said that JOA newspapers wanted to "sneak this [SA 2509] through without publicity, without hearings...in a way that's absolutely abhorrent to democracy and a free press" (Milligan, 1988).

The new legislation helped consolidate efforts among opponents of JOAs and resulted in the formation of a network of JOA opponents led by Brugmann and the Association of Alternative Newsweeklies. The group began regularly monitoring legislative and regulatory activities related to JOAs and published and distributed notices and articles about JOA developments, including the applications, decisions, and other developments on JOAs in Detroit, Manteca, York, Miami, and other cities. The network also began distributing articles and research about the efficacy of the NPA and suggestions for its modification or repeal (Busterna, 1987b, 1988c; Picard, 1988b).

HOUSE JUDICIARY COMMITTEE OVERSIGHT HEARINGS

Increasing debate over the NPA attracted the interest and concern of Representative Jack Brooks (D-TX), who organized oversight hearings by the House Judiciary Committee's Subcommittee on Economic and Commercial Law on July 20, 1989.

The hearings focused on the effectiveness of the statute in serving its purposes and were sparked by Brooks' "misgivings" about the law in light of the closure of the *Miami News* and the dispute over approval of the Detroit JOA (Garneau, 1989).

The NPA was defended in the hearings by Morris B. Levin, an attorney who has represented nearly every JOA newspaper. Levin argued that the NPA "has worked well, and its exemption from the antitrust laws has been judiciously provided" (Levin, 1989). His views were echoed by newspaper financial analyst John Morton, who told the subcommittee, "The public has been and continues to be well served by the existence of joint operating agreements" (Morton, 1989).

The American Newspaper Publishers Association (ANPA), which had not participated in the 1986 debate over extending the scope of the NPA, sent its president, Jerry Friedheim, to represent the association. Friedheim said the ANPA continued to support the NPA, as it had during the original hearings 20 years earlier, but its members were divided. He indicated the ANPA would oppose repeal of the NPA, but would "not reject orderly consideration of possible enhancements or updating in the Act" (Friedheim, 1989).

The NPA faced attack from the majority of witnesses at the hearing, who cited a lengthy list of problems and weaknesses caused by the NPA. Many critics, including Bruce Brugmann, W. Edward Wendover, a suburban Detroit publisher and opponent of the Detroit and other JOAs, and Louis Mleczko, Newspaper Guild leader in Detroit, called for outright repeal of the NPA. Other witnesses included Robert G. Picard, James Norton of the Graphics Communications International Union, and William Boarman of the Communications Workers of America. They urged revisions that would more clearly stipulate and regulate the approval process of JOA newspapers, restrict closure of JOA newspapers; limit the antitrust exemption, and require significant disclosure of data from JOA newspapers.

The National Newspaper Association, which represents smaller daily and weekly newspapers, reiterated its opposition to the NPA by submitting a statement calling for repeal of the NPA as a "blatant piece of special-interest legislation, without public policy benefits" (Garneau, 1989).

The hearings produced no committee action on the NPA, but served as an impetus for the growing corps of newspaper publishers and labor union leaders who were becoming increasingly vocal in their opposition to the NPA.

H. R. 4970

Efforts by NPA opponents intensified in early 1990 when opponents of the Detroit JOA application redirected their energies to set up a national group, Citizens for an Independent Press, to take part in policy debates over the NPA.

Ed Wendover, publisher of a group of suburban Detroit newspapers and head of Michigan Citizens for an Independent Press—which had opposed approval of the Detroit JOA and challenged Attorney General Edwin Meese's approval of it in court—was selected to head the organization. Members of the group included Bruce Brugmann and Julie Swope, who headed the Citizen's Independent Newspapers Committee that had opposed the York JOA application (Garneau, 1990b).

The group retained the services of Washington, DC, attorney Jack A. Blum, who had been assistant counsel for the Senate antitrust committee during hearings on the NPA. Blum developed a strategy for the group that included pushing legislation for outright repeal, but maintaining a fallback position that sought specific changes that would protect non-JOA newspapers and limit the abilities of JOA newspapers to use their market power (Blum, 1990).

At its 1990 convention, the Association of Alternative Newsweeklies, backing the efforts of the president, Bruce Brugmann, passed a resolution asking for "a legislative reappraisal of the Newspaper Preservation Act." Brugmann admitted that "it's going to be difficult politically, if not impossible, to make JOAs go away," but he told the group that "we can put all kinds of restrictions that will help us operate more profitably, more effectively in our cities" (Fitzgerald, 1990).

By the summer of 1990 the group had gained significant momentum, along with the support of Representative Carl Pursell (R-MI), who introduced legislation, H. R. 4970 (Figure 4.4), to repeal the NPA.

The bill, 14 lines in length, called for repeal of the NPA, but stated that repeal would not apply to JOAs entered into prior to the NPA, thus allowing them to continue operating. However, the bill would remove the antitrust waiver, forcing newspapers to comply with antitrust law

Figure 4.4. H. R. 4970

A BILL

To repeal the Newspaper Preservation Act.

Be it enacted by the Senate and House of Representatives of the United States of America in Congress assembled,
SECTION 1. REPEALER
 The Newspaper Preservation Act (15 U. S. C. 1801-1804) is repealed.
SECTION 2. APPLICATION OF REPEALER.
 Section 1 shall not apply with respect to—
  (i) any joint newspaper operating agreement entered into before July 24, 1970, and
  (ii) any joint operating agreement with respect to which the Attorney General of the United States grants consent under section 4(b) of the Newspaper Preservation Act (15 U. S. C. 1801-1804) before the date of the enactment of the Act.

as outlined in the Tucson case, and would have a similar effect on JOAs started since that time.

Although full repeal of the NPA was the stated goal of Citizens for an Independent Press, the group indicated that if its effort failed, it would seek disclosure of JOA newspapers' finances, prohibitions on volume discounts for advertising, and limits on the ability of JOA newspapers to operate subsidiary newspaper ventures such as total market coverage weeklies (Meyers, 1990).

The bill lapsed with the 101st Congress without gaining a legislative hearing. As this book goes to press, proponents of the bill are unsure whether further action will be pursued.

5
Theory and Philosophy of the Newspaper Preservation Act

Congress passed the Newspaper Preservation Act in 1970 "in the public interest of maintaining a newspaper press editorially and reportorially independent and competitive in all parts of the United States" (Newspaper Preservation Act, 1970). The Supreme Court, in *Citizen Publishing*, permitted cost sharing joint operations only. The court-approved modified joint operation in Tucson permitted a cartel Sunday edition with a combination rate sold by a joint advertising sales staff.

However, Congress passed the NPA, which permitted price fixing and profit pooling all week long, to circumvent the decision in the *Citizen Publishing* case and over the initial objections of the Department of Justice.

Though never specifically addressing the point, Congress may have believed that allowing the full 7-day cartel operation and a few additional incidental cost savings under the NPA would be the difference between financial survival or the demise of joint operations. Thus, charitably interpreted, one might argue that the philosophy underlying passage of the NPA was to forego the benefits of economic competition Monday through Saturday in order to preserve the benefits of editorial competition throughout the week.

The analysis of this chapter will show that assumptions about economic harms and content benefits are not necessarily correct. Even though the NPA eliminates all economic competition between the cartel newspapers, it may still provide some positive benefit for economic performance, not only for the newspaper owners but for advertisers and the public as well. Although the price-fixing, profit-pooling and market division aspects of the NPA ought to degrade economic competition, they may not be any more harmful than a single-newspaper monopoly—if Congress is right and monopoly is the only alternative. Furthermore, the cost sharing attribute of JOAs may improve the overall economic efficiency of newspaper operations (of course, nearly all the cost sharing benefits of the NPA are available without the NPA). On the other hand, the apparent editorial competition maintained through the NPA antitrust exemption may not provide any significant amount of "better" news content.

Policy justifications for the Newspaper Preservation Act may take two general forms. The NPA may improve the economic performance of the newspapers involved and it may improve their content performance. This chapter will define these performance goals and discuss in theoretical terms whether the NPA makes improvements in these areas. Comparisons will be made between the economic and content performance of the current JOAs and the other options available: limited joint operations, single newspaper monopolies, joint monopolies, and competitive duopolies. "Limited joint operations" refer to the joint operations that would be permitted if the NPA was overturned, such as the modified agreement in Tucson (Appendix B), or under a modified NPA that disallowed Monday through Saturday cartel operations (see Exhibit 1 in Chapter 8).

However, before this analysis can take place, a short review of some of the special characteristics of the newspaper industry will introduce some concepts that will be used in the subsequent analysis.

SOME ECONOMIC CHARACTERISTICS OF THE NEWSPAPER INDUSTRY

The first step in assessing the economic performance of JOA newspapers is to define the market within which the performance takes place. This definition is crucial because it determines the level of competition that might be expected from other news and advertising media produced in the same geographical area, as well as from newspapers and other media that exist outside the local area. This potential competition not only might have an impact on advertising and circulation prices, but it might also affect the nature of newspaper content available to readers.

If newspapers face intense advertising and circulation competition from other media, as well as newspapers published in different localities, then the formation of a joint operation should not be expected to have much impact on economic and content performance. Whatever benefits competition would bring to these performance criteria would remain about the same with or without a JOA. On the other hand, if price and content competition from other media outlets is minimal, then the formation of a JOA would have a significant impact on the level of competition faced by the two newspapers. This would be particularly true if the JOA was not necessary to the survival of the two newspapers—if a limited joint operation or duopoly could have been used as an alternative to a full JOA.

The information available to assist in determining the boundaries of a newspaper market is limited, but fairly consistent. It supports the conclusion that newspapers operate in both a narrow geographic and product market. This means that newspapers face little competition in advertising and circulation pricing, or for nonadvertising content.

One relevant information source for coming to this narrow definition is court decisions in antitrust cases. Because the NPA is part of the antitrust law environment facing newspapers, how the case law speaks to the issue of the level of competition from other media is vital. The U.S. Supreme Court has spoken twice on the issue of defining the relevant market for daily newspapers. In both the *Times Mirror* and *Citizen Publishing* cases, the Court stated that the geographic market was a single county and the product market consisted only of daily newspaper copies distributed there (United States v. *Times Mirror*, 1967, 1968; United States v. Citizen Publishing Co., 1968; Citizen Publishing Co. v. United States, 1969). All other media were specifically excluded:

> The daily newspaper business is a distinct line of commerce and is a product separate and distinct from any other product. It has sufficient peculiar characteristics and uses which make it distinguishable from all other products.... Daily newspapers have a unique market for which there is no real substitute. (*Times Mirror*, 1967, p. 617)

After presenting this general statement about the relevant product market within which daily newspapers operate, the District Court in the *Times Mirror* case went on to present specific evidence on how newspapers differ from other media.

> [Daily newspapers] provide more, wider and deeper coverage of all news—international, national and local—than any other medium of daily news dissemination. They offer a combination of syndicated features, such as comics, columnists and cartoons, not carried by any other medium. They provide readers with current advertising in greater depth and detail than any other medium. (*Times Mirror*, 1967, p. 617)

The court then went on to define the relevant geographic market to be a single county. The District Court opinion in *Citizen Publishing* was far more long-winded regarding these market definitions. It devoted 122 paragraphs of its decision to distinguishing daily newspapers from all other media and came to the same definitions of the product and geographic markets as the court in the *Times Mirror* case. Both District Court decisions were affirmed by the U.S. Supreme Court.

The Supreme Court has not spoken on the definition of the market within which newspapers operate since these cases came up in the late 1960s. More recent decisions by lower courts have used the narrow definition approach. All five Courts of Appeals decisions from the 1980 to 1986 were consistent with the earlier Supreme Court decisions (Busterna, 1988a).

This narrow product market definition is reciprocated in cases involving other advertising media. For a recent example, in *Omni Outdoor Advertising, Inc. v. Columbia Outdoor Advertising, Inc.*, a U.S. Court of Appeals ruled that billboard advertising resided in a separate product market from newspapers and all other advertising media (Omni Outdoor Advertising v. Columbia Outdoor Advertising, 1989). The issue of the advertising media product market definition may be so settled in the law that the question was not even put to the jury in the *Omni Outdoor* case. The lower trial court judge had directed the jury to define the relevant product market as billboards alone, and this was upheld by the Court of Appeals.

The few empirical studies that have attempted to measure the market boundaries for newspapers have also found this narrowness. In a study of weekly newspapers, Blankenburg (1980) found that the distance to the nearest separately owned daily, weekly, shopper or radio station had no variable effect on the advertising price charged by the weekly newspapers. This finding suggests both a geographic market restricted to the city or town of publication and a product market consisting of newspapers alone. Furthermore, he found no evidence of competition between daily and weekly newspapers.

Busterna estimated demand functions for national advertising in daily newspapers using data from 1970 through 1985 (1987a). Eight other national media were considered: daytime network television, evening network television, spot television, magazines, newspaper supplements, network radio, spot radio, and outdoor. Product markets are defined by the cross-elasticity of demand with various possible alternative products (U.S. v. duPont, 1956, p. 404; Brown Shoe v. U.S., 1962, p. 325). There was no evidence of cross-elasticities between newspapers and the other media. Price changes in none of these alternative advertising media relative to newspapers were associated with changes in the quantity of national newspaper advertising space sold. This suggests that most national advertisers do not consider daily newspapers to be an effective substitute for any of the other media studied.

In an earlier study, Landon (1971) measured the effect of local television advertising prices and the number of local radio and television stations on the national, local and classified advertising prices in newspapers. He found that variations in these other media have no impact on any of the three types of newspaper advertising prices. He concluded "that the relevant market for newspapers can be limited to the newspaper business itself" (p. 81).

In addition to these scholarly studies, industry practice also seems to consider newspapers as operating in a narrow market. Advertising buyers select the various media based primarily on differing "communication factors" rather than relative price. We would expect relative price to be the primary factor if newspapers were good substitutes for other media. Communication factors include such things as the level of intrusiveness (television is high, newspapers are low), the ability to include a coupon in the advertisement (newspapers are excellent, broadcast and outdoor have no such ability), permanence of message (newspapers are good, broadcast is poor), the ability to provide detailed explanations (broadcast is poor, outdoor has none, newspapers are very good), and so on. This industry practice is documented in advertising textbooks that deal with the selection of media for the advertiser's message (Sissors & Bumba, 1989).

Because the collective evidence points to a narrow market definition for newspaper advertising, cartels created by the NPA should be expected to have significant effects on the level of competition in the affected local newspaper markets. In the extreme case, granting a JOA in a local market in which the two newspapers could still maintain separate pricing policies through a limited JOA or through duopoly eliminates effective competition (at least for the Monday through Saturday editions). This elimination of competition may have a large impact on advertising and circulation prices as well as the journalistic product. In the less extreme case, where the JOA prevents a single-newspaper monopoly from developing, there may still be a significant negative impact caused by the joint operation. As discussed in more detail later, the JOA can jointly price advertising in its two newspapers to effectively force advertisers to buy ads in both newspapers even when they wish to purchase an ad in only one.

The narrow relevant market definition suggests that antitrust enforcement in newspaper markets in which direct competition still exists ought to be tougher than for the typical industry where firms face more competitors. More is at stake in trying to maintain some competition in the local newspaper market by duopoly or a limited JOA that excludes price fixing and profit pooling except on Sunday. Instead, these potentially competitive newspaper markets enjoy the special NPA dispensation from antitrust intervention.

As paradoxical as this seems, there may be a reasonable justification for it. Some form of joint operation in competitive newspaper markets may make good economic sense if newspapers in these markets are "natural monopolies." A natural monopoly exists where the minimum efficient scale of production, in which economies of scale are fully captured, is so large that only one firm can efficiently operate in the market. In a natural monopoly market, a single-firm monopolist can provide all the product at a lower cost than any combination of two or more firms operating under competitive conditions. The typical example of natural monopoly would be any of the public utilities. Water service can be provided more economically when only one set of pipes goes into each house in a community.

If a single printing and distribution firm in a newspaper market is the most efficient producer, then the NPA may make some economic sense. The NPA would allow the weaker newspaper to continue publishing with one combined, efficient production firm, rather than to be sold to the stronger newspaper or cease to exist altogether.

Two structural characteristics of newspapers do seem to cause them to act as natural monopolies. First, fixed costs are high and variable costs are low for newspapers. Second, the newspaper industry has a high degree of vertical integration where there is common ownership of both those stages of production that have high fixed costs and those stages that have much lower fixed costs. Both these structural factors contribute to natural monopoly and a justification for the production cost savings of joint operation.

Fixed costs are those costs that the firm incurs before the first copy of a newspaper is published. They remain constant over the production run for the newspaper. Fixed costs such as the printing plant building and equipment, delivery trucks, office space, and nearly all labor costs must be paid before the first copy rolls off the presses. Variable costs are the costs associated with producing additional copies of the newspaper. Additional copies require newsprint, ink, and incremental increases in other minor expenses.

Fixed costs for a newspaper are high while variable costs are low. This results in constantly decreasing average costs as additional copies of the newspaper are produced. The newspaper with the largest circulation in a market can then operate at lower average production costs than its smaller competitor. This places the newspaper with the smaller newspaper at a disadvantage, where it generates less profit or incurs losses because of the higher costs, pressuring the market toward a more efficient monopoly.

Parenthetically, the significant economies of newspaper production are another argument for a narrow definition for newspaper geographic markets. If newspapers had no reason to be narrowly geographically bound, we would expect only one general interest newspaper to exist in the United States instead of the over 1,600. Newspapers serve small geographic areas for two reasons. Obviously, in the extreme case, higher costs associated with far distant distribution would overcome the scale economies. More importantly, however, readers demand newspapers with geographically specialized content. Readers in San Francisco prefer San Francisco news to news of other areas. Furthermore, many readers in Marin County, although just across the Golden Gate Bridge, want a more local newspaper to cover their communities rather than simply relying on the San Francisco newspapers that can give only spotty coverage of their hometowns.

Every product, including newspapers, has various stages of production from raw materials through production and final distribution to the end users. When a single firm owns each of these stages of production, a high degree of vertical integration exists. In newspaper markets, the owners of those stages with high fixed costs such as the printing and distribution facilities also own the relatively lower out-of-pocket fixed cost stages such as reporters who gather raw information and editors who decide what goes into the newspaper. As has just been shown, in a local market with two separately owned newspapers, the larger circulation newspaper can use its cost advantage in printing and distribution to drive the smaller newspaper out of the market. Yet, the reporters and editors at the smaller newspaper may produce a product that readers and advertisers would support if only it could be provided at a lower cost.

Joint operation is a means to capture the cost advantages of larger scale printing and distribution that can be shared by two editorial departments when they form a single entity to carry out these high fixed cost functions. By forming this printing and distribution subsidiary, the two newspapers also reduce their vertical integration so that the firm that owns the largest circulation newspaper need not be the only editorial department in town. Of course, the limited JOA captures these cost savings in essentially the same manner as a JOA cartel.

Another factor favors monopoly in markets that have more than one separately owned newspaper. Not only does the larger circulation newspaper have a cost advantage over its competitor, but it also obtains a disproportionate advertising revenue advantage as well.

Because advertising rates are determined primarily by circulation, the smaller newspaper will get a lower price for a given size ad than the larger newspaper. However, advertisers will typically purchase more space in the larger newspaper as well. Many newspaper advertisers place an additional value on selecting the newspaper that will reach the larger audience. At times they will run ads in the larger newspaper that are not run in the smaller. Thus, the advertising revenue market share will favor the larger newspaper to a greater degree than its circulation market share might suggest. A newspaper with 52 percent of the circulation in a market might receive 60 percent of the advertising revenue.

The disproportionately lower advertising revenue, coupled with the higher production costs, can create a vicious cycle for the smaller circulation newspaper that places it in a competitively weaker and weaker situation over time. A small circulation disadvantage leads to higher costs and significantly lower advertising space and revenue. With lower revenue and advertising space, the amount of nonadvertising space declines. This may lead to a new cycle of circulation losses with an even greater relative cost disadvantage and loss of advertising space and revenue. Such a situation as been described as the "downward spiral" of local market newspaper competition.

The downward spiral theory suggests that competitive newspaper markets are in a disequilibrium condition. As long as two newspapers stay close in circulation they can continue to compete. Once one of the newspapers slips in circulation share, however, the downward spiral works to move the market toward monopoly. Clearly, there are a few markets in which even newspapers with discrepant circulation shares can coexist in the long run. In these markets, such as New York, the newspapers are sufficiently differentiated in content that they appeal to different groups of readers.

With a few exceptions where differentiated newspapers are published in large cities, monopoly does appear to be the equilibrium condition. The NPA implicitly acknowledges this and provides an antitrust exemption that may allow some weaker competitive newspapers to continue publication.

The cost sharing components of JOAs, including the joint Sunday edition and combination advertising rate sold by a combined sales force, provide the cost reductions that make the participating newspapers more likely to avoid the escalating cost aspects of the downward spiral. This goes a long way toward ensuring the continued survival of both editorial departments and may be all that is needed in most JOA or duopoly markets. The price fixing and profit pooling components of JOAs provide protection against the declining revenue aspect of the downward spiral. There is no incentive for either newspaper to lower prices or incur additional costs in trying to steal circulation and advertising away from the other newspaper because both newspapers draw a fixed percentage of revenue from one shared pool.

On the other hand, a limited JOA still maintains competition for greater profits in the Monday through Saturday editions that could result, theoretically, in pricing so low as to threaten the survival of one of the newspapers. There are two reasons why this should not happen. First, the cost sharing in a limited JOA, plus the joint Sunday edition, gives each newspaper much wider latitude in pricing for the other days of the week that will still result in profitability.

Perhaps more importantly, there is no logical incentive for a newspaper in a JOA to price in this manner. It reduces the profits of the one newspaper that is pricing aggressively and does so for as long as the JOA partner newspaper stays in business. Very large losses should accumulate. If this newspaper eventually succeeds in driving the limited JOA partner out of business, the surviving newspaper no longer gets the benefit of cost sharing and so has an especially difficult time recuperating the substantial earlier losses.

ECONOMIC PERFORMANCE CRITERIA

The standards of economic performance applied to joint operating newspapers are the same as the standards applied to economic performance in any other product market. These standards are presented in several texts from the subdiscipline of industrial organization economics (Bain, 1968; Caves, 1987; Scherer, 1980). Although these texts suggest several major and minor criteria, three factors appear most important in assessing the economic performance of newspapers. They are allocative efficiency, technical efficiency, and equity.

In the simplest terms, allocative efficiency in a local newspaper market occurs when the newspaper earns no above-normal profits. Allocative inefficiency occurs when a newspaper has the market power to restrict output in the local market and thereby charge higher advertising or circulation prices. Typically, output can be restricted in two ways. First, a newspaper with market power can prevent another newspaper from entering the local market. Second, the newspaper can reduce its circulation or advertising space sold by charging prices that force some potential subscribers or advertisers out of the market. In this second case, the price increase more than makes up for the decrease in circulation or advertising space sold.

The policy question here is whether joint operation with price fixing and profit pooling makes newspapers more or less allocatively efficient than they would be if the joint operation were not permitted.

Without a cartel JOA, one of four alternatives would occur. First, the two newspapers involved could have a limited joint operation where many costs were shared but price competition remained, at least for six days of the week. Second, they could remain, or revert to, competitive duopoly newspapers. A third option is that one newspaper may purchase the other and continue to publish it as a separate newspaper (joint monopoly). Finally, one of the newspapers may cease to exist either by stopping publication or by merger into one newspaper (single monopoly).

One task in this chapter is to discuss what economic theory has to say about the relative effects of these various alternatives on the level of allocative efficiency. The next chapter will present empirical findings on the association between these various competitive situations and advertising and circulation pricing behavior, which are measures of allocative efficiency.

The second economic performance criterion is technical efficiency. The most technically efficient newspaper is one that can produce a finished product for readers and advertisers at the lowest possible cost. Here we are concerned with the question of whether cartel joint operating newspapers are lower cost producers than any alternative competitive arrangement (limited joint operation, duopoly, joint monopoly, or single monopoly).

Equity refers to how wealth is distributed among the participants in a newspaper market (advertisers, readers, and the newspaper itself). On an ideal level, equity is maximized when wealth is distributed evenly among all participants. As a practical matter, however, with an equal distribution of wealth, some participants may lose their incentive to produce wealth. As a result, the participants in the market may receive less wealth than under conditions of less equality. This dilemma underscores one of the philosophical differences between socialism and capitalism.

Nevertheless, we may wish to make the normative judgment that the ability of a monopolist or cartel member to redistribute wealth away from advertisers, as well as the buying and reading public, through the implementation of higher advertising and circulation prices, is an undesirable equity outcome. Scitovsky (1971) concludes that it is impossible to separate equity considerations (how wealth will be distributed) from efficiency considerations (how the production of wealth can be maximized).

It is possible to simultaneously take into consideration both elements of efficiency (allocative and technical) along with equity. This analysis is shown graphically in Figure 5.1 (Busterna, 1988e; Williamson, 1968). P_1 and Q_1 represent, respectively, the price and quantity bought or sold of either advertising or circulation in a newspaper

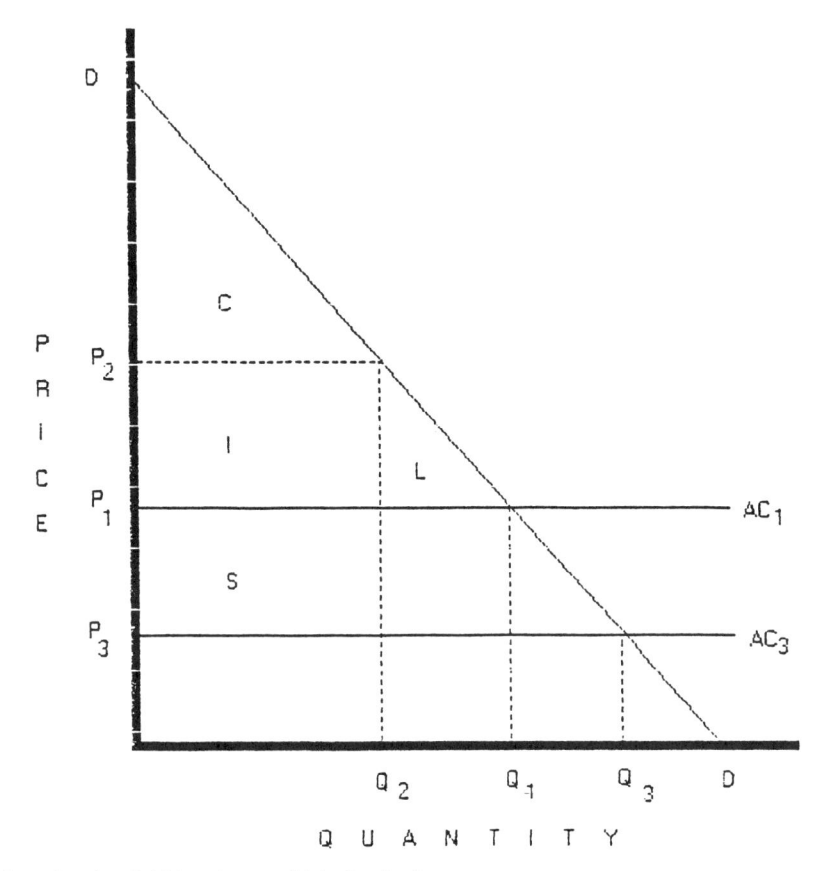

Figure 5.1. A Welfare Economics Model of Efficiency and Equity in Newspaper Markets

L = dead-weight loss from restricted output
I = income redistribution from consumers to producers
C = remaining consumer surplus after restricted output
S = cost saving through increased efficiencies

Figure adapted from "Economics as an Antitrust Defense: The Welfare Tradeoffs," by O.E. Williamson, 1968, *American Economic Review, 58*, p. 21. Reprinted by permission.

market. The newspapers are being produced with average cost AC_1. This set of price, quantity, and cost represents the first condition in a newspaper market associated with a given competitive situation (duopoly, joint operation, joint monopoly, or single monopoly).

The area consisting of $C + I + L$ represents the consumer surplus associated with the price, quantity sold, and average costs in this first condition. Consumer surplus consists of the utility that some consumers experience when the value they place on a product (reading or advertising in a newspaper in this case) exceeds the price they pay for it. Some advertisers or readers consider an ad or a copy of the newspaper, respectively, to be worth more to them than P_1. However, they only have to pay P_1 because that is the market-clearing price for all units no matter what value consumers place on them. The difference between what they would have been willing to pay (represented by demand curve DD) and P_1 represents the value of their consumer surplus.

Figure 5.1 also represents a second condition set of price, quantity, and consumer surplus. Here the price and quantity sold of advertising or circulation is represented by P_2 and Q_2. This second condition demonstrates greater allocative inefficiency relative to the first condition. The price for an ad or a copy of the newspaper is higher, and as a result fewer ads and less copies of the newspaper are purchased. Because the price now exceeds the value of advertising or reading the newspaper for some of the advertisers and readers in the first condition, they choose not to make a purchase. This results in a deadweight efficiency loss to total welfare, represented by the small triangle L. The advertisers and readers who pay the higher price redistribute a greater amount of money to the newspaper, represented by the rectangle I. The efficiency loss L and equity loss I are subtracted from the consumer surplus under the first condition, resulting in triangle C as the consumer surplus under the second condition.

This second condition is associated with a different competitive situation than the first condition. Traditional economic theory tells us that condition one represents a situation where there is some price competition among sellers in the market, whereas condition two represents a newspaper market in which there is no price competition between independently owned newspapers. Competition between two duopoly newspapers or two newspapers with a limited JOA might be expected to keep prices lower as in the first condition. On the other hand, because cartel JOA newspapers set joint advertising and circulation prices without any significant competitive forces from other media, these JOA newspapers have more control over prices so that they can be raised higher, as in the second condition. We would also expect joint-monopoly or single-monopoly newspapers to set prices according to the second condition. Thus, based on the analysis so far, allocative efficiency and equity would be expected to flourish under the more competitive newspaper market situations of duopoly or limited JOAs relative to cartel JOAs, or joint or single monopoly.

However, the theoretical analysis to this point has not yet considered technical efficiency. Improvements to technical efficiency in a newspaper market can increase consumer surplus. Figure 5.1 also represents a third condition with its own set of price, quantity, cost, and resulting consumer surplus. Here a change in the competitive situation in a newspaper market causes average cost to be reduced to AC_3. As a result of the reduced cost, the market-clearing price drops to P_3, from the original P_1, and the quantity of advertising or copies purchased expands to Q_3. Consumer surplus expands to the entire triangle bordered by AC_3, the vertical y-axis and the demand curve DD.

This gain in consumer surplus from increased technical efficiency has both an improved equity component and an improvement in total welfare. The rectangle bounded by AC_3, Q_1, AC_1, and the y-axis represents an income transfer to consumers (advertisers and readers) as a result of the cost saving. The triangle bounded by Q_1, AC_3, and DD represents the net welfare gain due to new advertising and readership brought on by the lower price.

Relative to the first set of conditions, this third set may represent the improved costs associated with producing newspapers under joint operation, either cartel or limited JOAs, or joint monopoly relative to duopoly. Joint operation or monopoly allows for the sharing of production, distribution, promotion, and other business expenses between two newspapers. This certainly means significant cost reductions over having these functions duplicated at each of the duopoly newspapers. Single-newspaper monopolies, as the result of merger or the failure of one newspaper, also result in technical efficiency improvements because a larger circulation single newspaper will have lower average copy costs than two smaller duopoly newspapers.

The preceding analysis shows that, theoretically, we might expect tradeoffs between allocative efficiency and equity on one hand, and technical efficiency on the other under different competitive conditions. Table 5.1 demonstrates that tradeoffs are involved when comparing nearly all of the different newspaper competition forms. Duopoly provides superior allocative efficiency and equity compared to cartel JOAs, joint monopolies, or single-newspaper monopolies. However, duopoly provides inferior technical efficiency relative to these other forms of competition. To make a good faith public policy decision among these options that already exist in daily newspaper markets (single and joint monopoly, duopoly, and cartel JOAs), an assessment of the empirical data is required. Unfortunately, we cannot directly assess the economic performance of limited joint operations, which appear to be the best theoretical public policy option, because they do not exist in actual newspaper markets. Chapter 6 will show that the meager empirical data provide less than desirable direction in measuring the tradeoffs.

Nevertheless, one unequivocal conclusion can be made that is not

Table 5.1. Forms of Newspaper Competition and Economic Performance

Newspaper Competition	Allocative Efficiency	Technical Efficiency	Equity
Limited JOA	Good	Good	Good
Cartel JOA	Poor	Good	Poor
Duopoly	Good	Poor	Good
Joint Monopoly	Poor	Good	Poor
Single Monopoly	Moderate	Moderate	Poor

subject to the vagaries of these welfare tradeoffs. On each of the three criteria of allocative and technical efficiency and equity, the limited joint operation provides equal or superior performance when compared to all alternative forms of competition, including the cartel JOAs that exist under the present administration of the NPA.

JOAs AND CONTENT PERFORMANCE

Because the stated intention of Congress was to maintain editorial competition, the net loss to economic performance that may be caused by the NPA could be counterbalanced by superior content performance. Congress may have believed that the NPA was necessary to maintain two editorial departments in cartel JOA markets, and that superior content performance would result. Chapter 6 will present some empirical evidence dealing with the question of whether two editorial departments produce a superior news and information product. Here the analysis will cover the more theoretical aspects of this question.

Congress' belief that two editorial departments are better than one stems from the long-held notion of the benefits of unfettered competition in the marketplace of ideas. This philosophy provides a powerful engine to the lore surrounding journalists and their practice. Members of Congress seemed to have put much value on it in attempting to justify the NPA.

In 1644, John Milton spoke of the evil of government censorship in *Areopagitica*. Yet, the same logic of finding truth from unfettered voices may be found by some to extend to the benefits of having more voices.

> And though all the winds of doctrine were let loose to play upon the earth, so Truth be in the field, we do injuriously by licensing and prohibiting to misdoubt her strength. Let her and Falsehood grapple; who ever knew Truth put to the worse in a free and open encounter? (Milton, 1951, p. 50)

Two centuries later, John Stuart Mill also appeared to support the notion that a diverse or, at least, unfettered marketplace is needed to arrive at truth. Like Milton, he did not use the marketplace analogy, but, more than Milton, he suggested that the public is better served by a debate over important issues affecting them.

> [Man] is capable of rectifying his mistakes, by discussion and experience. Not by experience alone. There must be discussion, to show how experience is to be interpreted. Wrong opinions and practices gradually yield to fact and argument: but facts and arguments, to produce any effect on the mind, must be brought before it. (Mill, 1977, p. 231)

In the 20th century, the Enlightenment notion of a diverse marketplace of ideas continues. According to Supreme Court Justice Oliver Wendell Holmes, the best test of truth is the power of thought "to get itself accepted in the competition of the market" (Abrams v. U.S., 1919). Thomas Emerson has written that a citizen

> must hear all sides of the question, especially as presented by those who feel strongly and argue militantly for a different view. He must consider all alternatives, test his judgment by exposing it to opposition, make full use of different minds to sift the true from the false. Conversely, suppression of information, discussion, or the clash of opinion prevents one from reaching the most rational judgment, blocks the generation of new ideas, and tends to perpetuate error. (Emerson, 1967, p. 7)

These concepts appear beyond reproach on an ideal level. Indeed, the basis for the First Amendment speech and press guarantees rests on these assumptions. Certainly, the philosophy has great validity when making extreme dichotomous comparisons. We would expect a press system with ownership spread across many private firms and relatively little government control to provide more beneficial content to the public than a totalitarian press system in which the government both owns and controls news and opinion content.

Unfortunately, our national political environment and journalistic practice itself may lead us to different conclusions about the diversity that a second newspaper may bring to the marketplace of ideas. With so little difference between the only two significant political parties in the United States, there is no demand for major newspapers to offer different news content or news values. The American public is substantially middle-of-the road, and so are its mainstream newspapers—those same newspapers that form JOAs.

Mainstream newspapers are motivated to please this centrist audience to maximize their circulation and, thus, their advertising revenue. As a result, mainstream newspapers make a great effort to look alike. Similar values in defining what is news, and the use of objectivity in covering these same news stories, results in so-called editorially competing newspapers that offer the public little difference in news and opinion.

Because newspapers must please the great body of the public in the middle, we should expect newspapers to passively let the government set the agenda and define the accepted position on these issues. Because the bulk of the public is satisfied with government, newspapers need not—nor dare not—take strong positions against the government. As a result we would predict that most news about the government would come from official government sources, and that countervailing forces would not offer fundamental criticism (Altheide, 1976; Cannon, 1977; Epstein, 1973; Herman & Chomsky, 1988; Roshco, 1975; Sigal, 1973; Tuchman, 1978). If newspapers are expected to rely so much on the same routine sources, then a second newspaper in a market should not be expected to add much diversity to the first.

Bigman, in one of the early empirical studies, suggests an economic class hypothesis for similar content.

> Publishers of the papers move in a social milieu which is much the same; their common attitudes are its product.... All the mechanisms of social control operate to keep the publisher in line with the opinion of those who constitute his social contacts.... The individual with sufficient capital to establish a new newspaper will, in all likelihood, merely offer one more voice to that part of the population already well represented in the press. (1948, pp. 130–31)

A more familiar study, published a few years later, fleshed out the mechanism whereby publishers can maintain control over the newsroom and, thus, the nonadvertising content of the newspaper. Breed (1955) found that publishers have a substantial ability to restrict the editorial policy of the newspapers they own. As did Bigman, Breed found that "policy usually protects property and class interests, and thus the strata and groups holding these interests are better able to retain them" (p. 334). We should not expect that the presence of two newspapers in a market, both owned by members of the same economic class, would offer any meaningful content diversity.

Objectivity is one of the cornerstones of American journalism. Whatever its virtues may be, objectivity leads to a lack of diversity in the way we can expect two newspapers to cover news. In Schudson's (1978) study of objectivity, he notes several criticisms. One is the process of news gathering which constructs an image of reality dependent on official sources. Another criticism is "that the content of a news story rests on a set of substantive political assumptions, assumptions whose validity is never questioned" (1978, p. 184).

Among these unspoken, but organic, values are belief in welfare capitalism, God, the West, Puritanism, the Law, the family, property, the two-party system, and perhaps most crucially, in the notion that violence is only defensible when employed by the State. (Newfield, 1974, p. 56)

Herman and Chomsky (1988) have also developed a similar theory regarding how unspoken biases shape the substantially monolithic mainstream news media. They note the following factors as leading to a conformist press with little meaningful diversity on important issues: size, ownership, and profit orientation of the news media; the need to obtain advertising revenue; reliance on a narrow set of official sources; criticism directed against media coverage; and anticommunism.

Just from this brief survey, it seems clear that simplistic Enlightenment notions of separate media voices leading to diversity in the marketplace of ideas is subject to question, at least as it applies to the issue of whether two daily newspapers in a market will perform better than one. We should not expect a second newspaper voice in a market to provide content diversity until one of two very significant changes occurs. First, the political environment in the United States must change dramatically. Until sizable groups of people lose faith in current newspaper coverage and demand different types of newspapers that better meet their own political biases, newspapers will be motivated to provide content that does not upset the current single mass of people in the middle. Second, newspapers themselves would have to decide to drop the standard of objectivity. However, this strategy is impractical because of the need to target a mass appeal product in order to maximize circulation and advertising revenue.

The foregoing analysis suggests that there is not much reason to believe that maintaining two editorial voices in a local daily newspaper market will improve content diversity. Yet, this content diversity standard is the stated purpose of the NPA. There may be an additional standard for assessing newspaper content performance. Quality, however difficult it may be to define, could be an unstated goal accomplished by the NPA.

A few empirical studies summarized in Chapter 6 attempt to define content quality by such measures as the amount of space devoted to nonadvertising content, the size of the news staff, the number of wire services purchased, and so on. Some controversy should be expected to surround any one measure of content quality. However, on a more abstract level, one factor seems to be in common among all these measures—they all seem to require a commitment of resources to the editorial product that raises the cost of producing the newspaper.

There is good reason to believe that the cartel nature of current

JOAs discourages the commitment of costly resources that would improve the quality of the editorial product. In theory, at least, the publisher of a duopoly newspaper may consider additional expenditures on the editorial product beyond some minimal level as a potential moneymaker. Putting more money into the editorial product may be motivated by a desire to steal circulation, revenue, and profits from the competing newspaper. Hopefully, this "capitalist" motivation to increase expenditures on nonadvertising material will coincidentally improve the quality of this material—however that quality may be defined.

This incentive, which may exist in a competitive newspaper environment of duopoly or limited joint operation, is foiled by the profit pooling aspect of a cartel JOA. There is no point in increasing editorial department expenses in order to steal circulation away from the competitor because there is no competitor. Cartel newspapers pool profits and then distribute them according to some preset proportion. Increased revenue for one of the cartel newspapers at the expense of its partner does nothing to increase the total pool. In fact, the added editorial costs of one of the JOA newspapers actually *reduces* its profits because these added costs must be subtracted from an unchanged revenue base.

Profit maximizing behavior for cartel JOA newspapers is to provide only a minimal editorial budget to prevent too many people from not buying a newspaper at all. The strong incentive to keep these costs at a minimum threatens the editorial independence of the two newspapers that the NPA was designed to protect. Because no increase in profits could result, the publisher of a cartel JOA newspaper may choose not to forfeit some of his or her own profits in order to serve some altruistic journalistic desire.

Cartel JOAs under the NPA should not be expected to have a significant impact on content diversity because of the greater market forces that create mostly undifferentiated newspapers. Furthermore, cartel JOA newspapers should not be expected to improve content quality, because the profit pooling feature of cartel JOAs creates a disincentive to spend beyond a minimal level for editorial costs.

With a limited joint operation, both newspapers maintain the same level of editorial competition and independence found in duopoly newspapers. Additional editorial expenditures may be viewed as a means toward greater revenue, which they cannot be in a cartel environment. A further investigation of the empirical evidence in Chapter 6 is needed to determine whether the possible preservation of a second editorial department in a city serves a useful purpose.

6

Empirical Studies of JOA Newspaper Performance

Chapter 5 has explained the difficulty in attempting to make *a priori* theoretical judgments about the economic or content performance of newspapers operating with joint agreements. Limited joint operations appear to have significant advantages over the cartel JOAs of the current Newspaper Preservation Act. However, it may still be helpful to see what light can be shed on this issue by reviewing the empirical evidence. Furthermore, unless the limited joint operation policy option is employed, "real-world" comparisons must be made among cartel JOAs, duopolies, single monopolies, and joint monopolies.

This necessitates an analysis of empirical studies to see how joint operating newspapers have performed in practice. Few such empirical studies exist that look specifically at joint operating newspapers. Unfortunately, some other studies combine JOA newspapers with other classes of newspapers (either monopoly or competitive newspapers) so it is not possible to isolate the impact of JOAs. This group of studies must be excluded from the analysis in this chapter.

Typically, the empirical economic studies have related various levels of competition to advertising prices. Their findings are somewhat complex and will be detailed. Several studies relate the quantity or quality of various types of newspaper content to the competitive environment. The preponderance of these studies shows that the content performance of joint operation newspapers, or even competitive newspapers, does not differ appreciably from single- or joint-monopoly dailies.

93

EMPIRICAL STUDIES OF ECONOMIC PERFORMANCE

The theoretical discussion in Chapter 5 suggested that limited joint operations should provide the best economic performance in terms of both minimum advertising and circulation prices and minimum costs. Unfortunately, because limited joint operations do not exist in actual newspaper markets, no empirical test of this proposition can be made directly.

However, evidence supporting limited joint operations can be developed indirectly if two results are found in the empirical research. First, we need to determine whether individual competitive newspapers price their advertising below that of individual cartel or monopoly newspapers. This provides evidence of allocative efficiency gains brought about by competition. Second, we need to find out if the combination rates offered by JOA cartels and joint monopolies are lower than the sum of the individual newspaper rates. This provides evidence of technical efficiency gains of joint operation or joint monopoly. If competitive newspapers demonstrate greater allocative efficiency and jointly produced newspapers have greater technical efficiency, then the marriage of these two advantages in limited joint operations would indicate an indirect empirical preference for them.

There are a few studies that compare advertising price levels between joint operating, joint monopoly, and duopoly newspaper pairs in local markets. Owen (1973) used multiple regression to study the combined national ad milline rate for 22 pairs of joint operating newspapers, 22 pairs of joint monopoly newspapers, and 12 pairs of competing newspapers. He found no difference in advertising price levels between joint operating and joint monopoly newspapers. As might be expected, newspapers in a joint operating cartel set advertising prices as if they were monopoly newspapers owned by the same company. On the other hand, the price for advertising in duopoly newspapers in the markets studied was significantly higher than the joint operation or monopoly newspapers' combined rates. Competitive ownership was associated with 13.5% higher advertising prices in cases in which space in both newspapers was purchased to display the same ad.

Lago (1971) used roughly the same set of newspapers at the same point in time as Owen, but added an additional independent variable to his regression model to control for circulation size. He used the combined flat ad rate as the dependent variable, which does not account for circulation size as does Owen's milline rate. He found no price differences among joint operating, joint monopoly, and duopoly newspapers. Clearly, the different form of the regression model affects the results of these first two studies.

Simon, Primeaux and Rice (1986) obtained results very similar to Owen's. As with the two previous studies, regression models were used with national ad rates. This study used the milline rate as in Owen's model but also included a circulation independent variable in keeping with the Lago model. The authors found that the combined ad rates for joint operating and joint monopoly newspapers were about the same, and that both these rates were significantly lower than the combined rate of advertising in the pairs of duopoly newspapers studied. An advertiser pays 20 to 30% less when buying a combination ad from a cartel or joint monopolist. This study went one step further by comparing the rates of buying in only one of the newspapers under each type of competitive situation. The authors found that the price for advertising in a single duopoly newspaper was 8 to 23% less than advertising in a single joint operating or joint monopoly newspaper. Again, there was no statistical difference between the prices for advertising in a single joint operating newspaper versus a single joint monopoly newspaper.

Matthews (1990) compared retail milline ad rates of 40 newspapers in all 20 JOA markets with 35 competitive and 50 "monopoly" markets. It was not reported whether these monopoly newspapers were single or joint, but no combination rate comparisons were made using the monopoly newspapers. Prices for individual monopoly newspapers were statistically equivalent to individual JOA newspapers, and both were statistically higher than individual competitive newspapers. However, the combination milline rate for pairs of JOA newspapers was less than the rate for individual monopoly and competitive newspapers ($p < .10$ for competitive newspapers).

Lago's results stand at odds with the other three studies. However, it is fairly certain that this disagreement is caused by the flat line rate used by Lago rather than the milline rate used in the other three studies. There is a strong reason to prefer the milline specification, since it more accurately measures the product that advertisers buy. Use of the flat line rate suggests that advertisers buy an ad of a given size irrespective of the audience that might see it. The milline rate acknowledges that the product that advertisers buy consists of both ad size and potential exposure to an audience of a given size.

The two studies that used the milline rate and made comparisons based on pairs of newspapers found that it is less expensive to buy ads in both joint operating newspapers than in both duopoly newspapers, and that joint operating and joint monopoly newspapers are priced similarly. The two studies that used the milline rate and made comparisons among individual newspapers found that it is more expensive to advertise in a single joint operating or joint monopoly newspaper than in a single competitive newspaper.

These empirical results suggest that the advertiser who wishes to purchase an ad in one of the two newspapers published in a market would get lower prices from a duopoly newspaper. On the other hand, an advertiser who wishes to run the same ad in both newspapers on the same day would get lower prices from joint operating (or joint monopoly) newspapers than from two duopoly newspapers.

From the downward spiral analysis in Chapter 5, we know that an appreciable number of advertisers do prefer to advertise in only one of two duopoly newspapers. But we also know from the experience of joint operating and joint monopoly newspapers that a significant number of advertisers do run the same ads in both newspapers. It would appear from the empirical evidence that it is not clear whether, on balance, advertisers are better served by joint operating or duopoly newspapers.

Another issue that complicates this judgment is that some of the advertisers who purchase ads in both joint operating newspapers may not be doing so out of their own choice. The advertising price structure of the typical joint operating agreement strongly discourages individual newspaper purchases. The joint operating newspapers in San Francisco provide an example of this. The open rate per column inch in the 562,887 circulation morning *San Francisco Chronicle* alone is $219. In the evening *Examiner*, the individual open rate is $141 for its 136,346 circulation (*Editor & Publisher International Yearbook*, 1991). However, the price for the insertion in the smaller *Examiner* can be reduced from $141 to $44 when purchasing the combination rate. Many advertisers who would have settled for a single purchase in the dominant *Chronicle*, which might be priced 15 or 20% lower if it was a duopoly newspaper, feel that the add-on cost of an ad in the *Examiner* is too good to pass up. The joint operating price structure seems to take away choice from some advertisers who would prefer a single ad in a lower-priced duopoly newspaper.

Even though some advertisers undoubtedly are forced into a combination purchased at a higher total outlay than the single ad they would prefer, other advertisers who really do wish to purchase space in both newspapers in a market benefit from joint operation. The overall impact of cartel joint operation on advertisers' welfare (and the welfare of the public that purchases the goods and services advertised) is indeterminate. Even an empirical investigation of the number of advertisers harmed and benefited by joint operation cannot resolve the question, because the price structure presented above masks the true number of advertisers who would choose to make combined purchases.

Specifically, it may be that the cost associated with printing the ad a second time in the other joint operating or joint monopoly newspaper is a good deal lower than the cost associated with printing the ad in the first newspaper. Much of this apparent cost savings may be passed on to the advertiser who buys a combination ad. Duopoly newspapers have separate advertising sales staffs and production facilities and so cannot capture the cost savings associated with the same ad placed in both newspapers. But again, joint monopoly or cartel joint operations are not the only means of capturing these cost savings. A limited joint operation would also allow a significantly reduced combination rate on top of individual newspaper ad rates that will be lower than their joint monopoly and cartel JOA counterparts.

This empirical evidence establishes the criteria necessary to indirectly show that limited joint operations would provide the best economic performance. Competition does reduce ad prices relative to a cartel or monopoly, but it cannot pass on any of the cost savings involved with placing the same ad in both newspapers that cartel or monopoly pairs can do.

Up to this point, the empirical studies have all dealt with static comparisons of advertising prices between newspapers in different competitive conditions. An important concern about the advertising price behavior of JOA newspapers is more dynamic in nature. What happens to advertising price levels over time?

For example, after the JOA was approved between the previously competitive daily newspapers in Detroit in late 1989, the anecdotal evidence from the trade press states that advertising and circulation prices soared. Advertisers and agencies reported some increases of over 200%. "Although agency sources say the actual rates haven't changed that much, they say the papers have adopted a strict policy of sticking to the rate card" (Strnad, 1990). Two weeks after the JOA was formed in Detroit, circulation prices also were raised significantly. The *Free Press* price rose 25% and the *News* rose 67% for the daily editions. The new, jointly published Sunday edition price rose 33% ("Price Hike in Detroit," 1989).

This information is startling on two counts. First, it suggests that studies ought to compare before and after advertising price levels to get a better idea of the impact of the loss of competition in newly formed JOA markets. Second, it suggests a significant flaw in all price studies. If competitive newspapers are more likely than joint monopoly or cartel JOA newspapers to negotiate prices lower than the printed rate card, then all the empirical studies overstate the actual competitive newspaper ad prices. Competitive newspapers may actually be performing much better than the evidence suggests.

The four static empirical studies summarized above are complemented by two dynamic studies of JOA newspaper pricing over time. Again, however, these studies may also overstate the actual ad prices charged by competitive newspapers. Picard and Fackler (1984) found that between 1972 and 1982, 40 JOA newspapers studied raised their national milline rates by 269%, while the 38 duopoly newspapers studied raised their milline rates by 166%. In 1972, the milline rate for ads in single JOA newspapers averaged 30% more than single duopoly newspapers. By 1982, the differential was 80%.

This study showed that JOA newspapers cause greater reductions in consumer welfare over time than duopoly newspapers. However, this study found that these reductions stem not only from greater increases in advertising prices over time, but also from significant reductions in circulation. The JOA newspapers in the sample experienced a 6.3% reduction in circulation, while the duopoly newspapers increased their circulation by 20.3%.

Price theory suggests that monopolists and cartels can restrict supply as a means of extracting higher prices and profits from a market. JOA newspapers can accomplish this by restricting circulation and raising advertising prices to a greater extent over time. Picard and Fackler found that these actions had occurred. They argue that duopoly newspapers are unable to use the same strategy because of their concern for the "downward spiral." Should one duopoly newspaper reduce its circulation in order to charge higher prices, it runs the risk of becoming the less desirable advertising vehicle.

Not only do the higher price increases over time by JOA newspapers harm the public, but reduced circulation does as well. In a different study relating circulation policy to type of ownership, Blankenburg (1982) found that Gannett, the nation's largest newspaper chain, significantly reduced the circulation of its newspapers compared to a matched set of newspapers owned by other companies. Blankenburg comments that

> In a way, circulation policy is a form of editorial policy, and withheld circulation is akin to suppressed information.... A small but interesting set of research has found an association between media richness and the level of information held by citizens [Stempel, 1973; Chaffee and Wilson, 1977; Clarke and Fredin, 1978]. Bereft of a newspaper or a choice among dailies, citizens may lack sufficient tools to exercise their [voting] franchise. (Blankenburg, 1982, p. 398)

Picard (1985), in a different study that used the same price comparison method over time, found that JOA newspapers raised their advertising rates 269%, while a set of single newspaper monopolies raised their rates 94%. Both of these studies across time periods show significant evidence of JOA advertising pricing behavior that is more harmful to consumer welfare than either duopoly or single newspaper monopolies—the most likely alternatives to JOAs if limited joint operations are not used. These two studies also found no differences in circulation pricing among competitive, JOA, and monopoly newspapers.

Overall, the preponderance of evidence shows that JOA newspapers provide inferior economic performance in the area of advertising pricing. The exception appears to be for advertisers who really wish to run the same ads in both local newspapers. JOA newspapers provide a lower combination rate for them as compared to duopoly newspapers. However, a single newspaper monopoly—the more likely alternative to JOAs than a duopoly—may well offer a lower ad rate to cover a local market's total daily newspaper audience than the combination rate of JOA newspapers that usually include undesirable audience duplication. Furthermore, the cost saving of the ad run in both cartel JOA newspapers would still exist with a limited joint operation.

EMPIRICAL STUDIES OF CONTENT PERFORMANCE

While the available empirical evidence on the price effects of JOAs is fairly sparse, the situation is no better for studies of content effects. The most common criticism of the NPA found in the literature is that it permits JOAs where a competitive duopoly would still have been possible (Barwis, 1980; Carlson, 1971). Of course, this criticism is directed more at how the NPA is administered than at the idea of JOAs themselves. At least for JOAs formed since 1970, the NPA specifies that joint operations can only be formed when one competitive newspaper in a market is likely to fail without it. Furthermore, these studies are found mostly in the legal literature, and they provide no new empirical evidence to support their criticism.

One study of JOA newspaper content found a very high similarity in the emphasis that same-market pairs of these newspapers give to various news story categories. Ardoin (1973) computed rank correlations for the space devoted to 10 news categories between 18 pairs of JOA newspapers. The rank correlations (Rho coefficients) ranged from .70 to .99, all significant at the .05 level, suggesting highly similar content in joint operations. The author of the study concluded, "Results of this investigation present a negative response to the question of whether joint printing newspapers maintain two different news voices in a community" (p. 347).

Given the theoretical argument of the previous chapter that virtually all general circulation dailies tend to be similar, it would have been interesting had this study included content comparisons within pairs of joint monopoly and duopoly newspapers. This analysis may have found that even a second duopoly newspaper in a market does not add a new voice.

Only a few empirical studies make comparisons between joint operating newspapers and newspapers in other competitive situations. Perhaps the earliest content study of joint operating newspapers was by Kearl (1958). He compared the proportion of joint operating, joint monopoly, single monopoly, and competitive newspapers with more than one major news service. Though he performed no statistical test himself, it is possible to perform t-tests for the difference between proportions on the data he provided. None of the differences in proportions involving joint operating newspapers was statistically significant.

Hicks and Featherston (1978) compared the Baton Rouge and New Orleans joint monopoly markets with the Shreveport JOA market. The study was limited by its case study scope, which prevents generalizability. Furthermore, the authors noted that the newspapers in Baton Rouge, the Louisiana state capitol, behaved differently from newspapers in the other two markets. By comparing the remaining pairs of newspapers, the authors found no differences in the amounts of duplication in each city. The joint monopoly newspapers in New Orleans and the JOA newspapers in Shreveport had about the same degree of duplication of news stories and neither pair had any duplication of editorials. Both pairs of newspapers devoted about the same proportion of space to nonadvertising material. This study presented one comparison in which JOA newspapers possess content characteristics very similar to joint monopoly newspapers, which is not consistent with the stated purpose of the NPA. The study suffers from a lack of comparison with pairs of duopoly newspapers.

A study by Litman and Bridges (1986) may have done the best job of comparing JOA newspapers with their most likely alternative under the present policy options, the single newspaper monopoly. In this study, four measures of "financial commitment" were used that should reflect on the general nature of newspaper content. They were full-time news staff, number of news services, lines of weekday news, and proportion of the newspaper devoted to news. Multiple regression models were developed for each of these dependent variables that included several noncompetition control variables. Individual joint operating newspapers were compared with single monopoly newspapers using a dummy variable approach. Joint operating newspapers did not have larger staffs, more lines of news, or a greater proportion of their newspapers devoted to news. They did average 1.34 more news services.

Although the statistically greater number of news services indicate greater "financial commitment" according to the authors' conception, this seems open to question. Additionally, more news services do not necessarily suggest greater *journalistic* commitment or quality. They may more likely suggest the opposite of both financial and journalistic commitment. Copy from news services is a relatively cheap way of filling the nonadvertising part of a newspaper. Thus, on three of the four criteria, JOA newspapers perform no better than single newspaper monopolies, and on the fourth they may perform worse. The authors concluded,

> The evidence presented gives no substantive support to the creation of joint operating agreements such as those created under the Newspaper Preservation Act. Neither is there any clear mandate favoring local newspaper monopolies.
>
> To be more precise: every time a market loses the stimulus associated with having two truly independent voices competing for the attention and financial support of the consuming public, the impact on the performance of whatever newspapers remain is expected to be either neutral or adverse. (p. 23)

Lacy (1988c) made content comparisons on 22 different categories between 21 competitive, joint operating, and monopoly newspapers. In the comparison between JOA and competitive newspapers, 17 of the 22 content categories were not statistically different. Competitive newspapers had a higher proportion of space devoted to news, more reporters, longer hard news stories, longer stories of all types, and a higher proportion of total editorial and op-ed space devoted to editorials. Because the competitive newspapers had higher average circulation, some of these differences may be attributable to circulation disparity rather than competitive environment. In the comparison between JOA and monopoly newspapers, 15 of the 22 categories showed no differences. Of the seven differences, monopoly newspapers actually had a larger proportion of the news section devoted to the news hole and fewer news services which is a dubious disadvantage. However, monopoly newspapers did have a smaller proportion of staff written copy. Perhaps because of the larger news hole generally, monopoly dailies had a smaller proportion of city and county news, more square inches per reporter, and a smaller proportion of space devoted to all editorial matter—the flip side of the monopolies' advantage in providing more news. With 17 of 22 content categories the same when comparing JOA and competitive newspapers, and 15 of 22 comparisons the same between JOA and monopoly newspapers, this is further evidence that there is not much content disparity no matter what competitive situation a newspaper faces.

Finally, White and Andsager (1990) found that JOA newspapers were more likely to win Pulitzer Prizes in the photography category than newspapers in other competitive situations. They also found that competitive newspapers were more likely to win Pulitzers in the national and international category as well as for commentary. Single newspaper monopolists did the poorest job in winning Pulitzers. From these results the authors concluded that there is a significant relationship between competition and winning Pulitzers—one measure of content quality. However, the study did not control for circulation size. Looking at the list of newspapers that win Pulitzers, it is clear that large circulation newspapers win disproportionately. Single newspaper monopolies are less likely to come from this group. Thus, failure to control for circulation invalidates the findings of this study.

Based on the preponderance of this small amount of empirical evidence, it does appear that, in most respects, JOA newspapers do not provide content performance any better than that which we would expect from joint or single newspaper monopolists. This should not come as much of a surprise given the discussion in Chapter 5 about journalistic conventions that tend to make most general appeal daily newspapers look similar. A different, relatively more substantial, body of empirical work demonstrates, for the most part, that even competitive duopoly newspapers do not provide meaningful content diversity or quality over monopoly newspapers. If full-blown competitive newspapers have content very similar to monopoly newspapers, we can have no reasonable expectation that the NPA can improve content performance even if it does succeed in preserving a few newspapers.

The earliest studies that compared competitive duopoly newspapers with monopoly newspapers looked at the degree of relative duplication, often using the single case study approach. At issue was the question of whether a second independent newspaper voice in a market added significantly to the diversity of information available.

The earliest study of the degree of content duplication between competing dailies was by Nafziger and Barnhart (1946). It consisted of a case study of two former competing dailies in a Minnesota community that were merged in 1940. By the time of the merger, the news policies of the two newspapers were almost identical, with virtually the same news events reported in both dailies according to the authors. The authors argued that this lack of differentiation contributed to there being no reason for the continuation of two separate dailies.

Bigman (1948) reported the results of a case study comparison of the content of the two duopoly newspapers in Pottsville, PA. A quantitative content analysis was made of one week's copies in 1946. Comparisons were made in the proportions of space devoted to various categories of news. The findings were described as "monotonous in their sameness." The subjects of the individual news items was also described as offering "no evidence of dissimilarity." Bigman found that the second newspaper added no controversial local editorials. On the most controversial issue covered in the newspapers, labor relations, the two newspapers were monolithic. His qualitative analysis showed that a large proportion of news stories in both newspapers were found to be "verbatim twins after a sometimes rewritten first paragraph."

Although he acknowledged the lack of generalizabilty from his case study, Bigman did conclude that if Pottsville was typical "the individual with sufficient capital to establish a new newspaper will, in all likelihood, merely offer one more voice to that part of the population already well represented in the press" (p. 131).

Willoughby (1955) studied the two competing dailies in a small (population 10,987) Indiana town. He performed a content analysis of four "representative" publishing days. In hard news categories (international, national, state and local news) the proportion of column inches devoted to items duplicated in the first newspaper ranged from 41% to 95%. One newspaper wrote three editorials, the other wrote four in the period studied. The author observed that the editorials seldom editorialized and they avoided controversial topics. The author further concluded that one writer's editorial columns provided more opposing viewpoints than all the other columns of both newspapers combined. More than 80% of local items of community interest, or "socialization" news, was duplicated. The author concluded that the "dailies not only resemble each other in makeup, typography and size, but also are very much alike in content. There seemed to be no essential differences between the two, and during the period covered two competitive daily newspapers did not appear to be necessarily better than one" (p. 204).

Another older study by Borstel (1956) went beyond the single-instance case study and looked at the content of 20 dailies, both duopoly and monopoly, all in communities with less than 25,000 people. Content analysis was employed over a six-week period. Three of the four pairs of duopoly newspapers showed no tendency to compete on issues or ideas. The monopoly newspapers were more likely to publish indigenous comment than the competing newspapers. Letters to the editor appeared least frequently in the competing newspapers. Within the pairs of competing newspapers studied, one daily tended to have a higher proportion of indigenous comment than the other. Though the author did not comment on these findings, they do suggest content performance in competing newspapers that is no better, and appears generally worse, than that of monopoly newspapers in the sample of small newspapers studied.

Nixon and Jones (1956) were the first to employ a relatively large sample of newspapers for their content study. The authors compared proportions of space devoted to 17 news categories among two data sets. They found no differences in the first data set and only one in the second with competitive newspapers averaging 0.85% more space to accidents and disasters. Rank correlations of .97 and .98 were found between the relative space allotments given to the 17 categories in competitive and monopoly newspapers in the two data sets. Although competitive newspapers had a slightly larger proportion of the total newspaper devoted to news in both data sets, the differences were not statistically significant. The authors concluded in conjunction with the earlier studies that there are no significant content differences between competitive and monopoly newspapers.

Similar to Nixon and Jones, Kearl (1958) used matched samples of newspapers under different competitive conditions. He was concerned with whether the number of major news service subscriptions differed across the competitive situations. Kearl reported no statistical tests in his article, but subsequent t-tests for the difference between proportions can be performed on the results he reports. For the smallest circulation dailies, under 15,000, competitive newspapers did subscribe to a statistically greater number of news services. In the circulation group above 40,000, there were no significant differences between JOA, monopoly, and competitive newspapers.

Rarick and Hartman (1966) also used a single newspaper case study approach, but they analyzed the same newspaper over time when it changed from a monopoly to a duopoly newspaper. They were particularly concerned with two questions: (a) Does competition encourage a larger proportion of nonadvertising content to originate locally? and (b) Does it encourage a larger proportion of its news and features to be devoted to sensational and human-interest content? Contrary to the previous studies, Rarick and Hartman found significantly more local (51% vs. 41%) and sensational (30% vs. 22%) content when competition was intense. Many will think that the second difference, the increase in sensational content, represents a relative disadvantage for competitive newspapers. Furthermore, one local content category, editorials, showed a significantly greater percentage under the monopoly condition, presumably another advantage for monopoly. This study should thus be viewed as giving a split verdict on the content performance of competitive and monopoly newspapers.

As with some of the previous studies, the Rarick and Hartman study concerned only one instance. Generalizations thus are not possible and some degree of apparently contradictory results are to be expected. Indeed, this appeared to be the case a few years later when Schweitzer and Goldman (1975) replicated this single-instance longitudinal design with a different newspaper. Contrary to the first longitudinal study, the findings here showed that during the period of intense competition the paper actually had a lower proportion of local content, although the difference was not significant. There were also no significant differences in the proportion of sensational content. The authors concluded that contrary to the Rarick and Hartman anomaly, "The findings of this study confirm the results of earlier studies in which it was found that the content of competitive papers is much the same" (p. 710).

Lacy (1987a) has criticized the Schweitzer and Goldman replication. Both longitudinal studies made comparisons at three points in time: no competition, weak competition (when the second paper trailed significantly in circulation), and intense competition (when circulation was close). Lacy claimed that Schweitzer and Goldman really did not compare a period of intense competition comparable to Rarick and Hartman. This raises the issue of whether intensity of competition is an appropriate measure for the purpose of assessing policy options toward newspaper competition.

Although this distinction in the level of competitiveness is useful to our understanding of the impact of competitiveness on content, it is not relevant to the policy question of whether the presence of a second newspaper improves content performance. Antitrust policies such as the NPA can only facilitate the presence of a second newspaper. It can do nothing to make the level of competition intense. Thus, in evaluating the value of the NPA in improving content, we should look only at the presence or absence of competition, not its degree of intensity. Furthermore, because the NPA is designed to preserve newspapers that would otherwise cease to publish because they are failing, we should expect the level of competitiveness in JOA markets to often be weak and, indeed, the circulation discrepancies of many JOA pairs bear this out.

The differences found by Rarick and Hartman were for the comparison of intense competition with no competition. When only weak competition was present, content was much more like the no competition period. This policy perspective diminishes the Rarick and Hartman result and gives added credence to the Schweitzer and Goldman findings of no difference in content accounted for by the presence of competition.

A third, more recent, longitudinal case study was performed on the *Winnipeg Free Press* by Candussi and Winter (1988). The *Free Press* became a monopoly in 1980 when its competitor, the *Winnipeg Tribune*, ceased publication. Two randomly selected constructed weeks were selected one year before and three years after the monopoly was created. With the monopoly, news hole increased significantly from 33% to 38%. The proportion of local to total news increased nonsignificantly from 22% to 24%. The number, proportion and length of local stories remained the same. The number of national and international stories did decline significantly. The usefulness of these results are harmed by the fact that the monopoly year studied, 1983, was a time of significant economic recession. The quantity of advertising sold was much lower than in the competitive year. Thus, the increase in news hole as a proportion of total newspaper space is affected by the sharp decrease in advertising. In the same way, the decrease of national and international stories reflects to some appreciable degree the loss in the absolute amount of space available to news. This unfortunate use of a recession year makes it difficult to interpret the mixed findings of this case study.

This problem is seen more clearly in another study of two newspapers that changed from competitive to monopoly status. McCombs (1988) also studied the *Winnipeg Free Press*, but in this study 1981 was used as the study year for the monopoly condition. This was a healthier year economically for the paper and the results bear this out. After becoming a monopoly newspaper, the *Free Press* increased the proportion and the *size* of its news hole. The only significant changes after monopoly were an increase in letters to the editor and a greater emphasis on local news with much more local staff-generated stories— all improvements in content performance. All the other content comparisons made showed no differences. In the other market studied, the *Montreal Gazette* significantly increased its general news, sports and comics after monopoly. It showed decreases in crime news and human interest material and an increase in political news, all of which suggest an improvement after the monopoly. The *Gazette* showed more emphasis on national news. It increased the number of stories written by the local news staff. Again, all the other content comparisons made showed no differences. McCombs found the competitive newspapers in both cities to be very similar to each other, describing them as "rivals in conformity." The results actually provide support for the idea that monopoly improves content performance.

A fifth study also used a longitudinal approach, this time on a sample of 78 daily newspapers. Grotta (1971) compared content changes in newspapers that changed from competitive to monopoly with newspapers that either stayed competitive or monopolistic throughout the time period studied. Using a multiple regression technique that controlled for circulation and retail sales, he found no significant differences between the two groups on five content-oriented variables: change in the number of editorial employees per 1,000 circulation, change in size of news hole, change in the proportion of local to total news, change in the size of the editorial page news hole, and change in local to total editorial content. Thus, the change to monopoly status was not found to lower these measures of content performance. This result on a relatively large sample casts greater doubt on the generalizability of the Rarick and Hartman case study finding.

Wanta, Johnson, and Williams (1990) performed a sixth longitudinal study in which they looked at content changes in one newspaper, the *St. Louis Post-Dispatch*. They looked at content at three points in time: in 1986 when the *Post-Dispatch* was in a JOA with the soon-to-collapse *Globe-Democrat*, in 1989 when there was no other daily publishing in St. Louis, and 1990 when it "competed" with the upstart *St. Louis Sun* that was soon to cease publication. Of course, there wasn't much change in the level of competitive intensity between any of these three time periods. Nevertheless, the research design sought to identify content measures that either increased or decreased moving from the JOA stage to the monopoly stage and then reversed direction when the competitive newspaper entered. Over 170 content measures were compared. Only the human interest news, political coverage, three headline point sizes, and the proportion of two-line headlines changed in a manner consistent with a competition effect. A more likely explanation for the change in political coverage was that the two "competitive" years had presidential elections (1986 and 1990) and the monopoly year was not an election year (1989). The changes having to do with headlines seem inconsequential.

Weaver and Mullins (1975) analyzed the content and format differences among 46 competitive newspapers published in 23 cities. Their approach was to make comparisons between circulation-leading newspapers as a group to the trailing newspapers. The comparisons were based on the proportion of the total nonadvertising space devoted to 22 different categories of news, as well as nonadvertising content, as a proportion of total newspaper space. At the conventional .05 level, they found no statistical differences between the two groups of newspapers in any of these categories. The authors also looked for format differences such as the number of columns per page, number and size of photographs, and headline size. Again, they found no significant differences. The leading newspapers were found to subscribe to more news services, 3.7 to 2.6. As with the Litman and Bridges study (1986), it is difficult to interpret this one difference in content performance. More news services may present additional, new material for the newspaper, but it is also a source of cheap nonadvertising content.

A more recent study by Entman (1985) compared single monopoly newspapers with competitive newspapers across nine different content measures. For eight of the nine comparisons no differences were found, and the ninth was barely significant. The author combined joint monopoly and joint operating newspapers together so that JOA dailies' content was not analyzed separately. Entman found no differences in the proportion of staff-written stories [here he assumed that more news service copy is bad, in contrast to Litman and Bridges (1986) and Weaver and Mullins (1975)]; the proportion of stories in which two or more "actors" were mentioned; the proportion of conflict stories in which two or more actors disagreed; partisan imbalance in news stories; partisan imbalance on editorial pages; liberal stands in editorials; focus on economic problems; and praise or criticism. The barely significant difference found competitive newspapers with a higher proportion of stories devoted to national and international problems, 44% to 38%. Given that nine tests at the .05 level were being made, there is a substantial likelihood that one would be barely significant even if the underlying data were random.

Three recent studies purport to find some significant differences in content performance between competitive and monopoly newspapers that set themselves apart from the overwhelming verdict of the rest of the literature (Kenney & Lacy, 1987; Lacy, 1987a, 1990b). The 1990 study found competition to be associated with a greater number of news service subscriptions. The Kenney and Lacy study found competition to be associated with the greater use of graphics and color. Lacy's 1987 study found no content differences associated with competition for 16 of 21 catagories analyzed, which does not do much to further the weak case that competition is a significant factor in affecting newspaper content.

All three of these studies used cross-sectional multiple regression models that appear to suffer from the serious flaw of multicollinearity. Both 1987 studies used the same data set, in which monopoly newspapers have an average circulation of 29,501, whereas the average circulation for competitive newspapers is 292,981. Because the same method for drawing the sample was used in the 1990 study, we should expect the same magnitude of circulation discrepancy between monopoly and competitive newspapers. With nearly all of the monopoly newspapers having significantly less circulation than nearly all of the competitive newspapers, the effects of the competition and circulation variables cannot possibly be separated. Other multiple regression studies of newspaper competition effects have used samples in which monopoly newspapers have circulations closer to competitive newspapers to avoid this potential multicollinearity problem (Busterna, Hansen, & Ward, 1991; Ferguson, 1983; Lago, 1971; Landon, 1971; Litman & Bridges 1986; Owen, 1973; Simon, Primeaux, & Rice, 1986).

The final problem with these three studies is the specification of the competition variable. Competition is measured as a continuous variable represented by the difference in circulation share between newspapers in a market (ranging from 0 for two newspapers in a dead heat to 1 for a single newspaper monopoly). This formulation treats a given circulation gap between pairs of competitive, joint operating, and joint monopoly newspapers the same. Differing levels of circulation disparity may give publishers of *competitive* newspapers an incentive to have different content. However, this is not true for JOA and joint monopoly newspapers because their publishers have no financial incentive to steal circulation from one another. Joint monopoly newspapers are owned by the same company, and joint operating newspapers share revenues according to a predetermined ratio. Therefore, the so-called intensity of competition formulation measures circulation disparity but not competition. Because we need to study the effects of different types of newspaper competition rather than merely circulation disparity, the competition variable must be expressed in categorical terms rather than as a continuous variable.

Taken as a whole, the empirical evidence comparing the content of competitive and monopoly newspapers shows almost no meaningful differences. The rare study that finds a few differences shows most comparisons still to be null. In addition, most of these contrarian studies appear to have some serious methodological flaws. The role of competition in affecting the content performance of daily newspapers is virtually nonexistent. Other factors that cause newspapers to be so much alike must be overwhelming any impact that competition might have.

SUMMARY OF FINDINGS

Empirical studies that have focused on the economic performance of JOA newspapers have compared advertising prices. Four studies used a cross-sectional approach looking at advertising prices across large samples of newspapers under differing competitive conditions at one point in time. Two studies looked at advertising price changes over time.

The three cross-sectional studies that included joint monopoly newspapers all showed that JOA newspapers charge the same price level as the joint monopoly newspapers. The three studies that expressed advertising prices on a cost per unit of circulation basis found that the combination rate for JOA newspapers was lower than the total price for running an ad in both duopoly newspapers in the typical market. These two findings suggest that JOA cartels do set prices in the same manner as a monopolist would, but there are cost savings involved in a combination buy that are enjoyed by the advertiser. Nevertheless, purchasing an ad in one JOA newspaper was found to be more expensive than the same ad in an equivalent duopoly newspaper. Furthermore, the anecdotal evidence and the findings of two studies that measured advertising price changes over time found that JOA newspapers raise prices faster than duopoly or single monopoly newspapers.

The policy implication from these findings is that the cost sharing component of JOAs does provide a real economic performance benefit (the lower combination rate), but that price fixing and profit pooling cause economic harm (higher single-insertion rates). The solution, as far as maximizing economic performance is concerned, would seem to be a return to the joint operation form envisioned by the Supreme Court in the *Citizen Publishing* case.

The overwhelming weight of the empirical evidence on the content performance of JOA, competitive, and monopoly newspapers shows great similarity, both in terms of diversity and quality. These findings lend substantial support to the sociology of news literature discussed in Chapter 5, which states that factors such as professional conventions overwhelm any possible effects of competition in forming the nonadvertising content of daily newspapers. Based on this theory and the empirical evidence we are left with no reason to believe that the NPA will provide the superior content performance implied by its goal to "maintain a newspaper press editorially and reportorially independent and competitive."

The economic theory and empirical evidence suggest that limited joint operations hold the best hope for maximizing economic performance. The empirical evidence and one prevailing theory (the sociology of news) suggest that newspaper competition has no appreciable effect on content performance. Thus, the limited joint operation appears to be the best policy option. No support is found for the current policy of allowing some newspapers a special exemption from the antitrust laws to form price fixing and profit pooling cartels for all seven days of the week.

7
Failures of the Newspaper Preservation Act

As mentioned briefly in earlier chapters, the Newspaper Preservation Act fails substantially in its intent to save newspapers, even preexisting JOA newspapers.

The primary reasons for newspaper mortality come from the advantages that one newspaper gains over its competition because of advertiser preferences for the largest circulation newspaper in a given market and the greater economies of scale enjoyed by the larger newspaper (Picard, Winter, McCombs, & Lacy, 1988; Rosse, 1967; Rosse & Dertouzous, 1979). The operations of JOAs do not ameliorate the first problem, but they do allow the newspapers to share benefits of economies of scale.

Joint operations and the NPA also do not remove financial and economic incentives for the dominant newspaper to become a monopoly (Busterna, 1987b; Patkus, 1984). Because a newspaper can reap more profit in a monopoly situation, leading newspapers benefit most by not entering a JOA if the alternative is that a secondary newspaper will fold shortly. If, however, the secondary newspaper is strong enough to prolong its demise—and through competition reduce the profits of the leading newspaper—there is incentive for the dominant newspaper to enter an agreement.

Entering such an agreement, however, does not mean that the leading newspaper loses its incentive to achieve monopoly status. Although newspapers typically make greater profits under a JOA, there still remains an economic incentive for the dominant partner to

111

take steps to ultimately dominate and refuse to renew the agreement with the weaker partner.

This is possible because entering and operating in a joint arrangement does nothing to improve the market position of the second newspaper. In fact, when the arrangement places managerial control in the hands of the dominant newspaper, the dominant newspaper typically ensures that the secondary newspaper is not allowed to engage in campaigns to significantly improve its circulation or advertising market position.

The demise of newspapers in JOAs has led publishers, industry observers, and policy makers to recognize that renewal and perpetual continuance of a JOA is not probable in most locations in which one newspaper dominates the other. As a result, publishers, especially those from major newspaper chains, have begun seeking changes in their agreements to prepare for the eventual closure of one of the newspapers.

In 1986, for example, Scripps-Howard simultaneously sold its *Evansville Press* and purchased the *Evansville Courier*. In doing so, the newspaper chain sold the subordinate newspaper and purchased the larger, dominant newspaper, protecting itself against the real possibility that the JOA will not be renewed when it expires in 1998. In the same transaction, Scripps-Howard bought the Evansville Printing Company, the joint venture firm of the two JOA newspapers, and took direct control of the shared business activities of the JOA (Fitzgerald, 1986). Although the Department of Justice investigated the arrangement, it ultimately permitted the sale to take place.

In a move designed to strengthen the owners of two JOAs, Gannett and E. W. Scripps in 1986 simultaneously renegotiated existing agreements in Knoxville and El Paso. The unusual restructuring took place after Scripps threatened that its *Knoxville News-Sentinel* would not renew its agreement with Gannett's *Journal*, which trailed in circulation by nearly a 2 to 1 margin. Refusal to renew would have undoubtedly led to the demise of the *Journal* because economies of scale and circulation-advertising disparity problems would have made it virtually impossible to survive separately.

In the restructuring, Gannett agreed that the morning *Journal* would switch publication cycle with the evening *News-Sentinel*, giving the Scripps newspaper the preferential publication time and making it more difficult for the secondary newspaper to improve its market position. In exchange, Scripps agreed to extend the Knoxville JOA for 20 years and to increase Gannett's ownership of the joint operating firm from 22.5 to 25% (Radolf, 1986a).

At the same time, the two newspaper firms agreed to alter provisions of their El Paso agreement. Gannett's *El Paso Times*, which led the *Herald-Post* 55,000 to 32,000 in daily circulation and operated the 86,000 circulation Sunday edition, was given half interest in the Newspaper Printing Corporation and an undisclosed increase in profit share.

As the new agreements were negotiated, rumors emerged that Gannett wanted to sell its weak *Knoxville Journal* and would do anything to extend the JOA and make it a marketable commodity. When the renegotiated agreements were announced, Gannett officials would not respond to questions about a potential sale. After the agreements in Knoxville and El Paso were restructured, however, Gannett sold the *Journal* to Persis Corporation.

The JOA newspapers in Birmingham have also altered their agreements in response to changing conditions and the dominance of one newspaper. Newhouse's dominant *News* was able to arrange a switch of publication cycle so that it will move to morning publication while Scripps-Howard's *Post-Herald* moves to the evening cycle.

In San Francisco, managerial differences have arisen between the partners and, despite the JOA, the *Chronicle* has experienced poor financial performance in recent years (Rapaport, 1989). Indicators have been observed that the Hearst Corporation, owner of the *Examiner*, wishes to purchase the *Chronicle* (Redmond, 1989). Many observers believe the JOA will be renewed in 1995 because of a clause that permits either party to force renewal, but the managerial disputes between the owners may still lead to changes in the agreement.

FAILED AND DISSOLVED JOAs

Concerns over the future of JOAs are not without basis given the closure of five joint operating newspapers and the dissolution of three other agreements. This section will discuss the demise of the agreements and newspapers separately.

The JOA failures that resulted in the closure of newspapers occurred in Columbus, OH; St. Louis, MO; Miami, FL; Shreveport, LA; and Tulsa, OK. Each presented increasingly complex and disturbing issues about the efficacy of JOAs as well as the NPA's effectiveness.

Columbus

On December 31, 1985, the Columbus, OH, *Citizen-Journal* published its farewell edition, becoming the first JOA newspaper to cease publishing. The newspaper died when its agreement with the competing *Dispatch* expired and Scripps-Howard executives determined that it would be unprofitable to keep the *Citizen-Journal* alive by establishing a new printing plant and operating it separately.

Scripps-Howard officials were aware that renegotiating the agreement would be difficult, and had been informed in 1982 that the *Dispatch* did not intend to renew ("Joint Operating Agreement May Be Terminated in Ohio," 1983), mainly because it wanted to shift to morning publication ("Columbus Dispatch Defends Ending of Joint Arrangement," 1983). In 1983 Scripps-Howard unsuccessfully offered to buy the *Dispatch* to keep both newspapers publishing. Although it was the morning newspaper, the *Citizen-Journal* trailed the *Dispatch* 200,000 to 117,000 and advertisers favored the *Dispatch*. Scripps-Howard executives blamed the failure on the refusal of the *Dispatch* to renew the agreement, despite offers to decrease the revenue share of the *Citizen-Journal* and to switch the secondary newspaper to an evening publication cycle. "It came down to a simple fact: the *Dispatch* will make more money without a JOA," the company's magazine reported ("What Went Wrong in Columbus," 1986).

In a final effort to gain something from the newspaper, Scripps-Howard placed the *Citizen-Journal* up for sale, but received no offers from newspaper companies. Finally, a local businessman agreed to purchase the *Citizen-Journal* prior to its closure, but backed out of the deal when he was unable to procure sufficient financing, facilities, and equipment to publish the newspaper.

"We can't be naive and assume that what happened in Columbus can't happen elsewhere," said Lawrence Leser, president of Scripps-Howard, after the closure. "But we continue to believe in joint operating agreements and feel good in the knowledge that our existing agreements will not expire for quite some time" ("What Went Wrong in Columbus," 1986).

St. Louis

In November 1983, the Newhouse newspaper company announced that it would close its *St. Louis Globe-Democrat* at the end of that year, leading the Department of Justice to assert that the newspaper could not be closed without its approval and a search for alternative buyers. The decision to shut down the newspaper fell outside the NPA's antitrust exemption and thus the joint decision to end the operation was subject to the requirements of the failing firm test ("St. Louis Daily in JOA Announces It Will Shut Down," 1983).

The decision to shut the Newhouse paper came after a number of years of operating losses. Although the *Globe-Democrat* had a slight circulation lead, Pulitzer's *Post Dispatch* enjoyed greater prestige and the Newhouse newspaper was operating at a loss. The decision to close the *Globe-Democrat* accompanied an amendment to the JOA that continued division of profits from the *Post Dispatch* between the two JOA firms until the agreement expired after the *Globe-Democrat* ceased publishing and was not transferred to another party who might wish to keep publishing the newspaper.

The requirement that potential buyers be sought before closure was approved resulted in the sale of the *Globe-Democrat* and its rocky operation as a competitor outside the JOA until the newspaper ultimately ceased publication October 29, 1986, when it could not overcome the structural difficulties that promote one-newspaper towns (Fitzgerald, 1984; Sanders, 1988).

Miami

The closure of the *Miami News* on December 31, 1988, in many ways paralleled the closure of the *Globe-Democrat*. The decision to close the newspaper if an alternative buyer could not be found was announced a week after Cox Enterprises and Knight-Ridder, owner of the *Miami Herald*, amended their JOA. The amended JOA gave Cox payments until 2021, whether or not the newspaper continued publishing, and precluded the JOA from being transferred to another publisher if the *News* was sold (Radolf, 1988).

The amended agreement would cost Knight-Ridder between $165 million and $500 million in payments to Cox, depending upon whose estimates were accepted. However, the costs were far lower than the costs for continuing to operate the *News* at a loss borne by the *Herald* (McPhail, 1988).

Potential buyers were kept at bay because of the late October announcement of the intent to sell the *News* before December 31 or shut it down, combined with its poor market position and lack of equipment and facilities since the JOA agreement was not transferable.

The manner in which the newspaper was killed, essentially a payoff by Knight-Ridder to Cox, disturbed many observers (Achenbach, 1989; Christensen, Dewar, & Ward, 1988; McPhail, 1988; Scardino, 1988). Although the Department of Justice indicated that the amended plan was under review, it did not halt closure of the *News* pending the outcome of its investigation. The newspaper ceased publication as planned. As of the writing of this book, the Department of Justice never completed or announced the results of its investigation and has taken no action against the Knight-Ridder and Cox agreement.

Shreveport

Announcement that the Shreveport JOA would cease operations on March 31, 1991, came as no surprise to many observers who had expressed concern about the ability of the *Journal* to renegotiate its contract that expired in 1994. In the decade prior to the demise of the newspaper, the afternoon *Journal* lost nearly half of its circulation.

The owner of the *Journal* was told that Gannett's *Times* would not renew the agreement in Spring 1990, but negotiations over the demise of the *Journal* kept the information confidential until February 1991. Under an agreement worked out between the JOA newspapers, the owner of the *Journal* ceased publication three years prior to the end of the agreement in exchange for an agreement that the *Times* would publish a second editorial page, edited by the *Journal*'s owner until December 31, 1999 (Fitzgerald, 1991).

Tulsa

The joint operating agreement between the *Tulsa Tribune* and the *Tulsa World* preexisted the Newspaper Preservation Act by 30 years, but neither its joint operations nor the NPA preserved the *Tulsa Tribune*, which ceased publishing September 30, 1992 (Case, 1992).

The paper was closed four years before the expiration of its agreement after managers of the joint venture, Newspaper Printing Corp., concluded that afternoon *Tribune* with only 67,000 compared to the *World's* 128,000 daily circulation was and would produce insufficient revenue to renew the agreement or permit the *Tribune* to operate independently after 1996.

In exchange for closing the *Tribune*, the *World's* owners agreed to pay the *Tribune's* owners's an immediate $11.5 million, plus $450,000 per month until the JOA's 1996 expiration date ($18,450,000), for a total deal worth $29,950,000.

In addition, the *Tribune* would receive 40% of the sales price of the assets of the Newspaper Printing Corp.

The three agreements that have ended with both JOA partners continuing to publish after the expiration of the JOA occurred in

Anchorage, Knoxville, and Franklin-Oil City. In Anchorage and Knoxville the JOAs dissolved to restore competition, but the Franklin-Oil City was dissolved as part of a buy out and merger of the newspapers.

Anchorage

The first failure of a JOA under the NPA occurred when the *Anchorage Daily News* left its joint operation with the *Times* after charging that the *Times*' dominance of the agreement resulted in managerial decisions designed to harm the secondary newspaper's ability to improve its market position. As indicated in Chapter 3, the *Daily News* did not collapse, because it gained capital and other financial resources through its sale to the McClatchy chain and has become a competitive operation once again.

Knoxville

Disputes between the parties in the Knoxville JOA in early 1990 led the E. W. Scripps Company to file suit against its partner for breach of contract. The suit arose after the Knoxville Journal Corporation, publisher of the *Journal*, acquired a daily newspaper in a satellite city. E. W. Scripps asked the judge to dissolve the JOA or order divestment of the Maryville-Alcoa *Daily Times* by its JOA partner, the Persis Corporation.

The E. W. Scripps-owned *News-Sentinel* dominates the Knoxville market with more than twice the daily circulation of the *Journal*, leading the chairman of the *Journal*'s parent company to charge that E. W. Scripps was looking for a way out of the JOA (Radolf, 1990). Ultimately, the dispute was resolved with an agreement for the newspapers to end their JOA on December 31, 1991, and for E. W. Scripps to pay Persis $40 million to compensate for profits the company would have received if the JOA lasted as scheduled, until 2005. Persis expected to continue publishing the *Journal* as a competitive evening newspaper after the agreement ended, much as the *Daily News* continued after the Anchorage JOA was dissolved (Garneau, 1990c; "Sentinel, Journal to End Agreement, 1990).

Persis, however, finally concluded that it could not operate the *Journal* as a daily newspaper and opted to change it into a weekly publication when the JOA dissolved ("Knoxville Journal," 1991).

Franklin-Oil City

The smallest JOA in the nation ceased operating in 1985 when the *Franklin News-Herald* and the *Oil City Derrick* merged. The consolidation occurred when Derrick Publishing Company purchased its JOA partner, the News Herald Publishing Company. This was the first time a newspaper purchased its JOA partner.

The purchase resulted in a Department of Justice investigation and the application of the failing firm test to the acquisition, the same test it had applied to the closure of the *St. Louis Globe-Democrat*. The Department determined that the *News-Herald* was a failing newspaper outside of the JOA but, unlike St. Louis, found that its owner had made reasonable efforts to seek another purchaser before selling to Derrick Publishing, and it approved the purchase and the ending of the JOA (Roper, 1985). Since the purchase, the *Derrick* now publishes a morning and an evening edition, but whatever editorial competition between the newspapers that existed under terms of the JOA has ended.

THE POTENTIAL FOR FUTURE FAILURES

The closure of JOA newspapers reveals that their operations and the NPA do not alter the forces promoting monopoly and do not ultimately work in saving newspapers. That such arrangements merely prolong the demise of newspapers and allow owners to draw profits from them for the protected duration of agreements has become well recognized and conveyed even in publications of the American Newspaper Publishers Association (Anderson, 1989).

Industry observers and critics of the NPA have begun using the evidence of changes in agreements and JOA failures—particularly the tactics used in the Miami failure—as arguments for revising or repealing the NPA (Henkoff, 1988; Peterson, 1990; Steel, 1989).

Three JOAs will expire during the 1990s and most observers expect that the secondary newspapers will experience extremely difficult negotiations for renewal or have renewal refused by the dominant newspaper in the agreement. The newspaper creating the most concern is the *San Francisco Examiner*, which has only about 20% of the daily circulation in its market. The *Evansville Press* is also seen as a problem because it has only about one-third circulation share in its market. Until 1992 observers were less concerned about the survival of the *Pittsburgh Post-Gazette* because it has maintained about 40% of the circulation share and its agreement did not expire until 1999. A prolonged strike in 1992, however, closed the Pittsburgh newspapers for much of the year and raised allegations that the E. W. Scripps Co. was trying to kill the *Post-Gazette* to leave the *Press* the only remaining newspaper in the city. Other observers stressed other factors as the cause of the labor dispute, but expressed concern that the strike will have changed advertisers' purchasing patterns and create an unrecoverable loss of advertising for the *Post-Gazette* after publication is resumed (Fisher, 1992; Fitzgerald, 1992).

Between the year 2000 and 2007, the agreements in Chattanooga and Cincinnati will expire and in the decade between 2010 and 2020 agreements in Birmingham, El Paso, Fort Wayne, Salt Lake City, and Tucson will end. Although it is far too early to project their futures, the current circulation share of the *Birmingham Post-Herald* is highly problematic and the shares of the *Cincinnati Post, El Paso Herald-Post*, and Salt Lake City *Deseret News* are within ranges of concern.

The inability of the NPA to significantly serve its stated goal of saving the nation's dying newspapers, and its inability to serve its real but unstated goal of protecting and saving preexisting JOA newspapers, makes it nearly impossible to maintain the argument that the NPA has been effective during its history.

8
Implications for Public Policy

The Newspaper Preservation Act provides an antitrust exemption that allows two separately owned newspapers in a city to form a price-fixing and profit-pooling cartel. Congress declared this exemption necessary in order to preserve editorial competition and independence. Previous discussions of public policy regarding the NPA have usually been centered on either supporting it in its entirety, or advocating the NPA's complete elimination. Because the NPA provides substantial profits for its beneficiaries, it is understandable to see newspaper industry advocates uncompromising in their support. Some elements of the newspaper industry, such as suburban or alternative weekly newspapers, are damaged even by the cost sharing element of joint operations. Again, their opposition to the NPA is understandable. However, the public policy discussion must overcome the self-serving interests of the newspaper industry and choose a path that maximizes the welfare of all.

Congress' action in enacting the NPA might be justified if the NPA met several conditions that would tend to maximize the welfare of all. First, the NPA should accomplish what its name implies—it should preserve newspapers. Second, it should accomplish its stated purpose of protecting and promoting editorial competition and independence. Third, it should maintain as much advertising and circulation competition as possible while still preserving as many newspapers as possible. Fourth, the NPA should maximize cost savings and mechanisms for encouraging newspapers to pass on much of this cost savings to their advertisers and readers.

A POLICY TO PRESERVE NEWSPAPERS

Chapter 2 provided a historical context for the ability of joint operations to preserve competitive newspapers throughout the 20th century. Chapter 7 provided a detailed case-by-case account of how specific JOAs failed to preserve the newspapers involved after the NPA was enacted into law. Neither account paints a successful picture of the NPA.

From 1910 to 1990, there was a decrease from 689 cities with competing daily newspapers to 21. While this represents a net decline of 668 cities with competing dailies, the newspapers in only 20 of these cities, 3 percent, have chosen to form joint operations. Since the first joint operation was formed in 1933, about 92% of cities with competitive newspapers have *not* chosen joint operation as a way of dealing with the loss of newspaper competition.

Chapter 7 recounted examples where newspapers in existing JOAs ceased publication (Miami, St. Louis, Columbus, Shreveport, Tulsa). One JOA ended when the two newspapers merged into one (Franklin-Oil City). Two JOAs broke up, although all four newspapers are still publishing competitively (Anchorage, Knoxville). Some JOAs may be dissolved in the near future, causing the possible loss of one of the newspapers in each cartel (San Francisco, Evansville, Pittsburgh). In the longer run, some problem JOAs may be emerging (Birmingham, Cincinnati, El Paso, Salt Lake City).

These problem JOAs taken together represent a substantial proportion of all JOAs that exist or that have existed. They demonstrate that the NPA has not been effective in preserving even those newspapers that chose to try to take advantage of the NPA's antitrust exemption. Of course, most competing newspapers, even in recent years, opt not to adopt a JOA in the first place and merge or cease publication instead. Between 1969 and 1986, 17 cities lost their competing newspapers but only two, Seattle and Cincinnati, opted to form JOAs. Since 1986, three new JOAs have been formed, but five existing JOAs have ended. Clearly, the NPA has not provided a successful means of preserving secondary newspapers in competitive markets.

Earlier chapters identified a key element of the NPA, or conventionally conceived joint operations before the passage of the NPA, that appears to prevent competitive newspapers from being preserved. The NPA requires that one of the newspapers must be failing before the antitrust exemption will be applied to a JOA. This works significantly toward discouraging two competitive newspapers from applying for a JOA in the first place. If the two competing newspapers operate separately until one of the newspapers has slipped so badly that it is truly failing, the dominant newspaper may choose to not form a JOA and simply wait for the weak newspaper to die. The dominant newspaper may feel that it can operate more profitably as a single newspaper monopoly than by sharing profits in a two-newspaper cartel. Or it may place greater weight on the noneconomic values of being the only newspaper in town, the victor, over an arrangement that maintains another voice in the market to dilute and compete with its own.

A good policy strategy, then, appears to be one that encourages joint operations to form before one of the competitive newspapers in a market is near collapse. In this manner, the beneficial effects of cost sharing in joint operations would likely be put in place before a clearly dominant newspaper develops in a competitive market. The theoretical analysis in Chapter 5, backed up with some empirical evidence in Chapter 6, showed that joint operations do indeed possess cost sharing benefits, and at least some of these benefits are passed on to consumers (advertisers, readers, and members of the public who buy products advertised in newspapers). Thus, it makes good sense to have a policy that encourages JOAs to form early, before one of the competitive newspapers falters too much and so that the public can begin to obtain the cost saving benefits of joint operation.

Some argue that one option might simply be to eliminate the failing newspaper requirement of the NPA. This would allow competing newspapers to form JOAs without having to go through the often long and costly process of showing that one newspaper is failing, or having to wait until a successful newspaper turns into a failing one.

However, even Congress did not advocate approving JOAs in markets in which both competitive newspapers were healthy. It is one thing to allow a newspaper that would have failed anyway to form a cartel with the dominant newspaper. The cartel eliminates competition, but competition would have been eliminated anyway if the failing newspaper had simply been allowed to cease publication. If both competing newspapers were still healthy, then allowing a cartel to form would eliminate competition at a time when competition was still feasible. Congress did not wish to go this far, and it is probably a good thing that they did not. A policy of letting viable competitors form cartels would violate the very essence of antitrust law and our reliance on free market economics.

Furthermore, providing an antitrust exemption to allow seven-day-a-week cartels does not appear to be necessary to permit joint operations that reap cost sharing benefits. A jointly produced Sunday edition does appear necessary to provide important cost-sharing benefits. Both competing newspapers in a market need a Sunday edition to survive. This requires a joint edition because the alternative is either doubling press and distribution capacity, which defeats the joint operation cost saving in the first place, or requiring one newspaper to publish a Sunday afternoon edition, which would seem to be an uncompetitive product to the partner's Sunday morning edition. Given that a joint edition is necessary to the survival of both newspapers, they must also be allowed to jointly set advertising and circulation rates for the Sunday edition and divide Sunday revenue in some agreed-upon manner.

However, although a joint Sunday edition is necessary to capture the cost sharing benefits of joint operation, the Monday through Saturday cartels permitted by the current NPA are not needed to capture any cost sharing. Partners in limited JOAs should be required to set advertising and circulation prices independently of each other, just as competing newspapers do, for the Monday through Saturday editions. The limited JOA partners could still share one advertising sales force to sell ads in both newspapers and the joint Sunday edition, and use a cost-justified reduced combination advertising rate that captures the cost savings of joint operation.

So, on one hand, good policy performance would benefit from the encouragement of the early adoption of cost-sharing joint operations at a time when both competing newspapers are still viable and more likely to want to form a joint operation. On the other hand, forming 7-day-a-week cartels at a time when competition is still feasible violates antitrust policy in a most fundamental way. The key to unlocking this dilemma is to allow the early adoption of limited joint operations that allow all of the important cost-sharing benefits to occur without permitting any unnecessary cartel operations that destroy the benefits of competition.

Limited joint operations that permit the full cost sharing aspects of JOAs under the currently formulated NPA, along with the joint Sunday edition, provide the kind of compromise position that avoids many of the problems the current NPA has with preserving newspapers. The joint Sunday edition is the only anticompetitive activity that is permitted. The Monday through Saturday editions will still be priced competitively, and the combination advertising rates should pass on some of the efficiencies to advertisers and the public.

This limited joint operation proposal was adopted in the Tucson market stemming from the *Citizen Publishing* case. The District Court that found full-blown JOA cartels to violate the antitrust laws permitted this type of limited joint operation to exist before the NPA exemption was law. This permission was granted to the two Tucson newspapers even though the court considered neither of them to be failing. Thus, we should expect that courts today would not find the limited joint operation, including the Sunday edition cartel permitted in the Tucson agreement, to violate the antitrust laws. Because the original intention of Congress in passing the NPA was to have an even more liberal policy than the courts toward joint operations, we should also expect that Congress would permit the early adoption of joint operations between two healthy, competitive newspapers that would occur with the limited joint operation policy.

The first element of a good and successful policy toward preserving competitive newspapers is that the policy ought to actually *preserve* these newspapers. Before the NPA was adopted, nearly all competitive newspapers that merged or ceased publication chose not to form full joint operations. One key element that prevents more full joint operations from being formed is the failing newspaper requirement. Limited joint operations can be legally adopted even when both competitive newspapers in a market are still viable, which should increase the likelihood that both newspapers would wish to adopt the joint operation. Thus, limited joint operations may be more successful in preserving competitive newspapers than the current NPA policy.

A POLICY TO PROMOTE EDITORIAL COMPETITION

A second element of sound public policy toward the preservation of competitive newspapers is that editorial independence and competition should be protected and promoted. Within the text of the NPA, Congress declared that the purpose of the law was "the public interest of maintaining a newspaper press editorially and reportorially independent and competitive." Further on, the text of the NPA states that joint operations between two newspapers can occur "provided that there is no merger, combination, or amalgamation of editorial or reportorial staffs, and that editorial policies be independently determined."

However noble the intention of trying to maintain editorial independence and competition, the discussion in Chapter 5 presented several reasons why we should not expect much editorial independence or competition even out of separately operating competitive newspapers. Privately owned profit-seeking newspapers will be highly motivated to provide the kinds of editorial content that will not upset the great mass of people in the political middle in the United States (the narrow band extending from liberal Democrats to conservative Republicans). Journalistic standards and practices would seem to draw all daily newspapers toward similar content.

The empirical studies summarized in Chapter 6 demonstrated that even separate competitive newspapers in the same market provide little content diversity. Empirical studies that measured content quality in a different manner, as the level of resources devoted to various editorial endeavors, also did not discover many meaningful differences even among competing newspapers.

A theoretical argument presented in Chapter 5 suggests that we should expect even less incentive for improved content quality to develop in JOA markets. A competing newspaper may consider greater expenditures on editorial improvements as a way of gaining an upper hand on its rival, resulting in stealing circulation away or providing an incentive to maintain its own readership. A cartel newspaper has no such incentive to spend money on the editorial product, because stealing readers away from its partner would not generate any increased revenue for itself and only increase its expenditures, detracting from the newspaper's own profits.

Cartel JOAs provide at least a *theoretical* incentive to perform worse than competitive newspapers, because the cartel creates a disincentive to spend money on editorial product. Shifting to a policy that permits only limited joint operations should not be expected to improve content diversity or quality in any meaningful way. After all, fully competitive newspapers do not offer significantly different content than monopoly or cartel newspapers.

However, with a policy of permitting only limited joint operations, the government will not be seen as taking a role in supporting the current cartel policy that provides a disincentive for the participating newspapers to spend additional resources on editorial quality. Limited joint operations will maintain full competition between the two joint operating partners for their Monday through Saturday editions.

If it were expected by the management of one of the newspapers in a limited joint operation that greater expenditures on the editorial product would steal some circulation away from its partner, then the newspaper enacting this policy could generate greater profits. They would have the same incentive to compete editorially with the other newspaper in town as any fully competitive newspaper has. The empirical evidence suggests that this incentive is not very powerful, but at least the public policy would be encouraging editorial competition. The current policy of permitting 7-day-a-week cartels under the NPA *discourages* editorial independence and competition. The proposed policy of limited joint operations provides the possible incentive to *encourage* editorial independence and competition.

A POLICY TO MINIMIZE THE LOSS OF ECONOMIC COMPETITION

The NPA says nothing about Congress' desire to maintain economic (advertising and circulation) competition. Presumably Congress would have wanted to maintain as much economic competition as was practicable while still preserving two newspapers in joint operations. However, Congress apparently thought that preserving any level of economic competition in joint operations was not possible.

Unfortunately, the NPA hearings ended shortly before the modified joint operation agreement was approved in Tucson. Had Congress kept the hearings open until the Tucson agreement was released, it would have seen that it was possible to have a joint operation with the full cost-sharing benefits of joint operations under the NPA, but with economic competition maintained for the Monday through Saturday editions.

This idea of a Sunday-only cartel was never considered by Congress in its NPA hearings so we do not know Congress' view of the policy. But it is difficult to see what kind of legitimate objection Congress would have had to the limited joint operation approved for Tucson. If Congress wished to oppose the limited joint operation and go forward with the 7-day-a-week cartel, they would have had to declare that the additional cartel profits from the Monday through Saturday editions were the one single factor necessary for the survival of both newspapers in the market. Because no members of Congress, nor any of the people who spoke in favor of the proposed NPA legislation, ever acknowledged that JOA newspapers earned extraordinary profits, it is unlikely that the bill's proponents, or members of Congress, would have used the argument that the extra profits from the Monday through Saturday cartel were necessary.

On one hand, some JOAs with 7-day-a-week cartels have failed with the weaker newspaper ceasing publication after the JOA was dissolved. Obviously, because a full cartel was not enough to keep these JOAs in operation, a more limited joint operation would not have kept both newspapers operating either. For these newspapers, the limited joint operation is no worse at preserving newspapers than the current NPA. On the other hand, in JOA markets such as Detroit, where the two partners are relatively close in circulation share, the substantial cost savings from joint operation coupled with the substantial profits earned from the Sunday edition would be more than adequate to make both newspapers profitable.

Current JOA newspapers will not like limited joint operations because they would naturally prefer to operate as a cartel every day of the week. Newspapers operating within limited cartels will earn somewhat smaller profits than current JOA newspapers. However, this extra profit now earned comes from cartel advertising and circulation pricing on the Monday through Saturday editions. The collusion used in pricing these daily editions is not necessary since the joint operating newspapers will still get the benefits of cost sharing, and advertisers and the public will get the benefits of a reduced combination advertising rate from a single sales force, even without the cartel. The only factor that changes is that the advertising and circulation pricing decisions will be made at each newspaper, as independently as it is now done at fully separated competitive newspapers. A policy based on a Sunday-only cartel will ensure as much economic pricing competition between two joint operating newspapers as is practicable while still preserving virtually all the newspapers publishing in JOAs under the current NPA. This policy will provide to advertisers and the public the benefit of competitively priced advertising, subscription, and single-copy rates, along with some of the benefits of cost sharing that should reduce prices even more than those available from full JOA cartels. It should be the rare, or perhaps nonexistent case, that finds this one difference to result in the collapse of a joint operation that would have continued if the daily cartel had been permitted.

A POLICY TO MAXIMIZE COST SAVINGS TO CONSUMERS

The fourth and final element of a policy to preserve second newspapers in competitive markets is that the policy should maximize cost savings *and* have mechanisms for encouraging newspapers to pass on much of this cost savings to their advertisers and readers. The current NPA does a good job of maximizing cost savings through joint operations where virtually all costs except those associated with each newspaper's editorial departments are shared. However, the NPA fails to provide the proper motivation (that is, competition) to pass on the maximum amount of these cost savings to advertisers and readers. The limited form of JOAs proposed here provides virtually the same level of cost sharing with a superior means of passing on the resulting savings to advertisers and readers.

Section 3(2) of the NPA found in Appendix A makes clear that a significant degree of cost sharing is permitted between two newspapers in a full-cartel JOA. Only the news and editorial functions of the two JOA partners are kept separate where no cost sharing is allowed. However, this same section of the NPA permits both newspapers to jointly set advertising and circulation prices on all editions of their newspapers and to pool all their revenues, both of which have nothing to do with improving cost savings except for the joint Sunday edition.

The empirical evidence in Chapter 6 indicated that full-cartel JOA newspapers pass on some of their cost savings from joint operations in the form of lower advertising prices for advertisers that place ads in both newspapers' Monday through Saturday cartel editions. On average it was found to cost advertisers more to place ads in both competitive newspapers in a market than in both JOA newspapers in a market, other considerations being equal. Thus, despite the negative aspect of JOAs possessing daily cartel operations that cause no greater cost savings, they did pass on some of the cost savings.

However, the empirical evidence also showed that the price for placing ads in individual competitive newspapers was less than the price of placing ads in individual JOA newspapers. This suggests that competitive pressures exist, even in two-newspaper markets, to reduce prices that are not present in JOA markets. With limited joint operations, competition would be restored to the pricing of ads in the Monday through Saturday editions, but cost sharing and a cost-justified combination advertising rate would also be permitted. Based on traditional economic theory and the empirical evidence, we should expect that the competitive pressure between the two partners in a limited joint operation should motivate them to provide even lower combination advertising rates than exist with the current cartel JOAs.

Limited joint operations provide the competitive mechanism necessary to motivate newspapers to pass on as much cost savings as possible. This leaves the question of whether limited joint operations generate as much cost savings as cartel JOAs. The limited joint operation permitted in Tucson by the federal district court in the *Citizen Publishing* case provides for all the essential cost sharing operations found in JOAs under the current NPA. Yet, there were a few areas in which the Tucson agreement did not provide the same level of cost savings. Limited joint operations can be given even more cost-saving opportunities that would make them virtually identical to cartel JOAs, but would still maintain the level of competition that the court sought in the Tucson agreement.

The Tucson agreement required that each newspaper maintain a separate advertising sales staff to sell noncombination ads that ran only in one newspaper (Section IIb). In practice, this did not seem to add any costs to the Tucson operation because only one salesperson was used by each newspaper to sell these individual ads, and this salesperson would have likely been employed by the joint venture firm if they were not needed at each newspaper. The rest of the sales force was run by the joint venture firm and sold combination ads in both newspapers and in the joint Sunday edition. However, limited joint operations do not need to maintain this single additional salesperson provided that the joint venture sales force is instructed to sell single ads in either newspaper "by the rate card" without any negotiation (which is what happens anyway in joint operations). This requirement guarantees that the individual newspapers are still independently setting their own advertising rates, but once this is done there is no anticompetitive effect in having the joint venture act as agent and sell single ads in either newspaper.

In the same vein, Section IIb of the Tucson agreement, reprinted in Appendix B, stated that each newspaper was individually responsible for its own advertising and circulation promotion. Maintaining daily edition competition between two limited joint operating partners requires that advertising and circulation prices be determined separately at each newspaper. Once this is done, it appears that competition is not harmed by having the joint venture firm act as agent for both newspapers in promoting advertising and circulation.

For example, once a newspaper has decided on its own that it would have a "two months for the price of one" offer to new home delivery subscribers, competition is not harmed by having the joint venture firm fill out new subscription orders for the newspaper or even to provide a bank of telephone callers to seek out new subscribers (whose time would be billed to the one newspaper).

Some advertising promotion will consist of marketing research studies or printed materials that can be used by the joint advertising sales force to convince prospective advertisers that newspapers are a more effective medium than radio or television. This type of promotion seems appropriate to the joint venture firm in a limited joint operation. Of course, if one newspaper wished to print a pamphlet that contained the proposition that it had more favorable advertising rates than its joint operating partner, it should pay for the cost of this item itself. Otherwise, nearly all advertising and circulation promotion could be handled by the joint venture firm without harming competition once the pricing decisions for the daily editions had been made individually at each newspaper.

By amending the Tucson agreement to allow the joint venture firm to sell all advertising, and to handle all advertising and circulation promotion, virtually all the cost savings available through full-cartel JOAs would also be available through limited joint operations. Whatever cost-sharing differences that might still exist would be negligible at most.

IMPLEMENTING LIMITED JOINT OPERATIONS

Because limited joint operations do not require one of the newspapers to be failing, they may be more successful in preserving newspapers than the current policy. Limited joint operations also provide a greater incentive to maintain editorial competition than cartel JOAs. Limited joint operations maintain advertising and circulation price competition for the Monday through Saturday editions. Lastly, limited joint operations possess all the cost savings of cartel JOAs and also provide for competition between the two partners for the daily editions, which should cause more of the cost savings to be passed on to advertisers and readers in the form of lower prices.

Two questions remain. Would Congress allow limited joint operations to replace the current NPA with its cartel JOAs? How can the new, limited joint operation policy be implemented?

Of course, trying to guess what Congress might do is difficult. On one hand is an obvious pragmatic argument against making the policy change. Current JOA newspapers will not like it because it will cause a decrease in profits. Several large and, presumably, politically powerful newspaper companies own JOA newspapers and they would be expected to lobby hard to protect profits. On the other hand, arguing in favor of full cartels over limited joint operations is difficult. No additional cost savings are involved. Virtually every newspaper that will be preserved with a full cartel will be preserved with a Sunday-only cartel. Newspaper companies that wish to argue in favor of the status quo may have to rely heavily on the argument that the press has the power to affect future elections. This may be a very successful strategy.

However, the change in policy to limited joint operations may have some success with Congress because it appears to change things so little. Past attempts against the NPA have concentrated on having it thrown out altogether. These attempts have relied on arguments that newspapers fail because of bad management or that there is no middle ground between competition and cartel. The limited joint operations policy accepts the arguments that most competitive newspapers markets will lose their competition over time, that joint operations do provide significant cost savings, and that maintaining a second newspaper is a good idea provided that it operates with the greatest amount of editorial and economic competition as possible. Congress need only agree to the proposition that Monday through Saturday cartels provide no cost savings and are probably not necessary to the survival of any newspapers. Furthermore, some elements of the newspaper industry may like the idea that lucrative joint operations can be formed without showing one newspaper to be failing, and without the time, expense, and uncertainty of going through the legal hoops of the current NPA.

The limited joint operation policy can be enacted in one of two ways. The first strategy would be to eliminate the NPA. Joint operating newspapers would simply enter into limited arrangements similar to the Tucson agreement, perhaps with the additional cost-saving steps mentioned above. Presumably the courts would permit these agreements if there was any legal challenge, as the federal court did in the

Citizen Publishing case. Joint operating newspapers might even get summary judgments and avoid litigation as long as their agreements really are limited and do not include price fixing and profit pooling for their daily editions.

Eliminating the NPA in order to enact a policy of limited joint operations poses two problems. First, it may appear to Congress to be a drastic measure which would encourage their opposition to it. Second, even if the NPA was repealed, some uncertainty would be created when the courts are left to settle the issue of the legality of limited joint operations. Extensive litigation might occur and there might even be contradictory decisions from different jurisdictions.

The second strategy for implementing a policy of limited joint operations appears more sensible. The NPA can be amended to disallow cartels for daily editions, but permit the rest of the activities of current JOAs. Congress may then see the minor change for what it is. By keeping the joint operation policy in statutory form, there is likely to be far less litigation and the policy could be uniformly applied.

Exhibit 1 reproduces the text of the Newspaper Preservation Act and then marks the deleted and additional words that would constitute an amended NPA that would permit only limited joint operations.

The first change in the amended NPA reflects the difference in the philosophy of the two policy options. The original NPA stated that the purpose was to provide an antitrust exemption for failing newspapers. The amended NPA does not require failure and encourages its cost saving provisions to be used by all competitive newspapers to preserve them before they become failures.

Section 2 drops a reference to existing joint operations that were created because of economic distress. Whether all existing JOAs at the time, as well as all new JOAs that have been formed since 1970, involve one newspaper that is in economic distress has always been a controversial issue. Many argued that in Detroit, for example, neither newspaper was failing at the time the JOA was approved. With a change to a policy of limited joint operations, the issue of whether a newspaper in a joint operation is truly failing is no longer relevant because all competitive newspapers, even those that are undeniably profitable, qualify for a limited joint operation.

Section 3(2) contains the most additions and deletions because it specifies the activities between the joint operating newspapers that will be permitted under the NPA. The added material specifies that a joint Sunday edition is permitted, as well as cost-justified combination advertising rates. Both of these activities are permitted under the current NPA. However, the remaining new language states that the joint price fixing of advertising and circulation rates and revenue distribution (profit pooling) is permitted only for the Sunday edition. This means that each newspaper must set its own advertising and circulation rates for the daily editions, a change from the current NPA.

The final change in Section 3(2) is to delete language that states that the two newspapers must keep their editorial functions separate. This provision may not be enforceable in the current NPA as it may be viewed as running afoul of the First Amendment. It is doubtful that Congress would deny the benefits of a JOA to two newspapers because of a problem Congress had with its news or editorial content. In any case, Congress certainly would not have this power to dictate editorial autonomy with limited joint operations. Because the *Citizen Publishing* case made it clear that limited joint operations were legal even without the NPA, and even between two nonfailing newspapers, Congress would violate the First Amendment if it forbade two competing newspapers to have a limited joint operation because of their editorial conduct. With limited joint operations, if the two partners wanted to combine some of their news staffs, Congress could not prevent them from doing so, just as Congress could not prevent competing newspapers from combining some of their news functions.

The definition of a failing newspaper in Section 3(5) is deleted because it is irrelevant to the amended NPA. Section 4(a) is also deleted because it relies on the failing newspaper distinction. Again, a phrase in Section 4(b) that refers to failing newspapers is deleted. Section 5 is completely deleted because it refers to providing litigation immunity to joint operations in effect before the original NPA was enacted, which is no longer relevant.

SUMMARY

This book began by defining joint operations within and outside of the NPA and providing a history of the development of JOAs and the NPA itself. A detailed account was given regarding how the NPA has been applied to requests for new JOAs as well as how newspapers have qualified for the NPA by being characterized as failing. Legislative attempts to alter the NPA were described. Chapter 5 described some of the economic theory underlying the newspaper industry and presented the economic and content performance criteria to be used in evaluating public policy directed at the newspaper industry. An analysis of empirical research indicated that competitive newspapers charge lower advertising prices, but that joint operations create cost savings that are partially passed on to advertisers. An analysis of the research on content performance showed that we should expect few differences in the content of competitive, joint operating, and monopoly newspapers. The many failures of the NPA to preserve newspapers were recounted next.

Finally, an argument was presented that limited joint operations are a superior policy alternative to the current cartel JOAs. Amid the swirl of the many attempts to extend the cartel powers of the NPA on one hand, or to eliminate them altogether on the other, only time will tell if a moderate policy course such as the limited joint operations proposed here will be adopted. In the meantime, competitive newspapers continue to cease publication and the continuation of many existing JOAs appears doubtful.

Exhibit 1:
Amended Newspaper Preservation Act

The actual NPA is reproduced below. The suggested amended NPA that would permit only limited JOAs consists of deletions shown as strike-throughs of the original text with additions shown underlined.

~~PUBLIC LAW 91-353—JULY 24, 1970~~

AN ACT

To exempt from the antitrust laws certain combinations and arrangements necessary <u>to preserve competitive</u> ~~for the survival of failing~~ newspapers.

Be it enacted by the Senate and House of Representatives of the United States of America in Congress assembled,

SECTION 1. This Act may be cited as the "Newspaper Preservation Act."

DECLARATION OF POLICY

SEC. 2. In the public interest of maintaining a newspaper press editorially and reportorially independent and competitive in all parts of the United States, it is hereby declared to be the public policy of the United States to preserve the publication of newspapers in any city, community, or metropolitan area where a joint operating arrangement has been heretofore entered into ~~because of economic distress~~ or is hereafter effected in accordance with the provisions of this Act.

DEFINITIONS

SEC. 3. As used in this Act—

(1) The term "antitrust law" means the Federal Trade Commission Act and each statute defined by section 4 thereof (15 U.S.C. 44) as "Antitrust Act" and all amendments to such Act and such statutes and any other Acts in pari materia.

(2) The term "joint newspaper operating arrangement" means any contract, agreement, joint venture (whether or not incorporated), or other arrangement entered into by two or more newspaper owners for the publication of two or more newspaper publications, pursuant to which joint or common production facilities are established or operated and joint or unified action is taken or agreed to be taken with respect to any one or more of the following: printing; time, method, and field of publication; allocation of production facilities; distribution; advertising solicitation; circulation solicitation; business department; <u>a jointly produced Sunday edition;</u> establishment of advertising rates

for the joint Sunday edition only; establishment of cost-justified combination advertising rates for advertisements purchased to run in both daily newspapers or either daily newspaper and the jointly-produced Sunday edition; establishment of circulation rates and revenue distribution for the joint Sunday edition only: *Provided*, ~~That there is no merger, combination, or amalgamation of editorial or reportorial staffs, and that editorial policies be independently determined.~~

(3) The term "newspaper owner" means any person who owns or controls directly, or indirectly through separate or subsidiary corporations, one or more newspaper publications.

(4) The term "newspaper publication" means a publication produced on newsprint paper which is published in one or more issues weekly (including as one publication any daily newspaper and any Sunday newspaper published by the same owner in the same city, community, or metropolitan area), and in which a substantial portion of the content is devoted to the dissemination of news and editorial opinion.

~~(5) The term "failing newspaper" means a newspaper publication which, regardless of its ownership or affiliations, is in probable danger of financial failure.~~

(5) ~~(6)~~ The term "person" means any individual, and any partnership, corporation, association, or other legal entity existing under or authorized by the law of the United States, the District of Columbia, the Commonwealth of Puerto Rico, or any foreign country.

ANTITRUST EXEMPTION

~~SEC. 4. (a) It shall not be unlawful under any antitrust law for any person to perform, enforce, renew, or amend any joint newspaper operating arrangement entered into prior to the effective date of the Act, if at the time at which such arrangement was first entered into, regardless of ownership or affiliations, not more than one of the newspaper publications involved in the performance of such arrangement was likely to remain or become a financially sound publication: *Provided*, That the terms of a renewal or amendment to a joint operating arrangement must be filed with the Department of Justice and that the amendment does not add a newspaper publication or newspaper publications to such arrangement.~~

SEC. 4. (a) ~~(b)~~ It shall be unlawful for any person to enter into, perform, or enforce a joint operating arrangement, not already in effect, except with prior written consent of the Attorney General of the United States. Prior to granting such approval, the Attorney General shall determine that ~~not more than one of the newspaper publications involved in the arrangement is a publication other than a failing newspaper, and that~~ approval of such arrangement would effectuate the policy and purpose of this Act.

EXHIBIT 1: AMENDED NEWSPAPER PRESERVATION ACT

(b) ~~(c)~~ Nothing contained in the Act shall be construed to exempt from the antitrust law any predatory pricing, any predatory practice, or any other conduct in the otherwise lawful operations of a joint newspaper operating arrangement which would be unlawful under any antitrust law if engaged in by a single entity. Except as provided in this Act, no joint newspaper operating arrangement or any party thereto shall be exempt from any antitrust law.

~~PREVIOUS TRANSACTIONS~~

~~SEC. 5. (a) Notwithstanding any final judgment rendered in any action brought by the United States under which a joint operating arrangement has been held to be unlawful under any antitrust law, any party to such final judgment may reinstitute said joint newspaper operating arrangement to the extent permissible under section 4(a) hereof.~~

~~(b) The provisions of section 4 shall apply to the determination of any civil or criminal action pending in any district court of the United States on the date of enactment of this Act in which it is alleged that any such joint operating agreement is unlawful under any antitrust law.~~

SEPARABILITY PROVISION

SEC. 5. ~~6.~~ If any provision of this Act is declared unconstitutional, or the applicability thereof to any person or circumstance is held invalid, the validity of the remainder of this Act, and the applicability of such provision to any other person or circumstance, shall not be affected thereby.

~~Approved July 24, 1970.~~

APPENDIX A:
Text of the Newspaper Preservation Act
Public Law 91-353—July 24, 1970
An Act

To exempt from the antitrust laws certain combinations and arrangements necessary for the survival of failing newspapers.

Be it enacted by the Senate and House of Representatives of the United States of America in Congress assembled,

SEC. 1. This Act may be cited as the "Newspaper Preservation Act."

DECLARATION OF POLICY

Sec. 2. In the public interest of maintaining a newspaper press editorially and reportorially independent and competitive in all parts of the United States, it is hereby declared to be the public policy of the United States to preserve the publication of newspapers in any city, community, or metropolitan area where a joint operating arrangement has been heretofore entered into because of economic distress or is hereafter effected in accordance with the provisions of this Act.

DEFINITIONS

SEC. 3. As used in this Act—

(1) The term "antitrust law" means the Federal Trade Commission Act and each statute defined by section 4 thereof (15 U.S.C. 44) as "Antitrust Act" and all amendments to such Act and such statutes and any other Acts in pari materia.

(2) The term "joint newspaper operating arrangement" means any contract, agreement, joint venture (whether or not incorporated), or other arrangement entered into by two or more newspaper owners for the publication of two or more newspaper publications, pursuant to which joint or common production facilities are established or operated and joint or unified action is taken or agreed to be taken with respect to any one or more of the following: printing; time, method, and field of publication; allocation of production facilities; distribution; advertising solicitation; circulation solicitation; business department; establishment of advertising rates; establishment of circulation rates and revenue distribution: *Provided,* That there is no merger, combination, or amalgamation of editorial or reportorial staffs, and that editorial policies be independently determined.

(3) The term "newspaper owner" means any person who owns or controls directly, or indirectly through separate or subsidiary corporations, one or more newspaper publications.

(4) The term "newspaper publication" means a publication produced

on newsprint paper which is published in one or more issues weekly (including as one publication any daily newspaper and any Sunday newspaper published by the same owner in the same city, community, or metropolitan area), and in which a substantial portion of the content is devoted to the dissemination of news and editorial opinion.

(5) The term "failing newspaper" means a newspaper publication which, regardless of its ownership or affiliations, is in probable danger of financial failure.

(6) The term "person" means any individual, and any partnership, corporation, association, or other legal entity existing under or authorized by the law of the United States, the District of Columbia, the Commonwealth of Puerto Rico, or any foreign country.

ANTITRUST EXEMPTION

SEC. 4. (a) It shall not be unlawful under any antitrust law for any person to perform, enforce, renew, or amend any joint newspaper operating arrangement entered into prior to the effective date of the Act, if at the time at which such arrangement was first entered into, regardless of ownership or affiliations, not more than one of the newspaper publications involved in the performance of such arrangement was likely to remain or become a financially sound publication: *Provided*, That the terms of a renewal or amendment to a joint operating arrangement must be filed with the Department of Justice and that the amendment does not add a newspaper publication or newspaper publications to such arrangement.

(b) It shall be unlawful for any person to enter into, perform, or enforce a joint operating arrangement, not already in effect, except with prior written consent of the Attorney General of the United States. Prior to granting such approval, the Attorney General shall determine that not more than one of the newspaper publications involved in the arrangement is a publication other than a failing newspaper, and that approval of such arrangement would effectuate the policy and purpose of this Act.

(c) Nothing contained in the Act shall be construed to exempt from the antitrust law any predatory pricing, any predatory practice, or any other conduct in the otherwise lawful operations of a joint newspaper operating arrangement which would be unlawful under any antitrust law if engaged in by a single entity. Except as provided in this Act, no joint newspaper operating arrangement or any party thereto shall be exempt from any antitrust law.

PREVIOUS TRANSACTIONS

SEC. 5. (a) Notwithstanding any final judgment rendered in any action brought by the United States under which a joint operating arrangement has been held to be unlawful under any antitrust law, any party to such final judgment may reinstitute said joint newspaper operating arrangement to the extent permissible under section 4(a) hereof.

(b) The provisions of section 4 shall apply to the determination of any civil or criminal action pending in any district court of the United States on the date of enactment of this Act in which it is alleged that any such joint operating agreement is unlawful under any antitrust law.

SEPARABILITY PROVISION

Sec. 6. If any provision of this Act is declared unconstitutional, or the applicability thereof to any person or circumstance is held invalid, the validity of the remainder of this Act, and the applicability of such provision to any other person or circumstance, shall not be affected thereby.

Approved July 24, 1970.

APPENDIX B:
Tucson Modified Joint Operating Agreement

The modified joint operating agreement in Tucson was entered on January 26, 1970, as the "Amended Order for Modification of Operating Agreement and Decree of Divestiture (1970 Trade Cases 88,278)." It remained in effect until superseded by the Newspaper Preservation Act on July 24, 1970.

The agreement consisted of five parts. The Order for Modification itself was published by the Commerce Clearing House (1970 Trade Cases 88,278). There were four attachments to this order that were not published with it. These were the (1) agreement between *Star* and TNI (Tucson Newspapers Incorporated, the joint venture company) providing for printing and distribution of newspapers by TNI, and for sales of combination advertising, (2) an identical agreement between the *Citizen* and TNI, (3) joint venture agreement for joint Sunday newspaper, and (4) revised by-laws of TNI.

The agreement between the *Citizen* and TNI and the joint Sunday newspaper document are reproduced here. They outline activities of the Tucson joint operation that were permitted by the Justice Department and federal district court from the *Citizen Publishing* case. Each newspaper must determine its own advertising and subscription rates Monday through Saturday. Otherwise, it is similar to other JOAs.

AGREEMENT

THIS AGREEMENT by and between CITIZEN PUBLISHING COMPANY, a corporation, publisher of the Tucson Daily Citizen, and TUCSON NEWSPAPERS, INC., a corporation;

WITNESSETH THAT:

WHEREAS Citizen Publishing Company, hereinafter called "Citizen," is the publisher of Tucson Daily Citizen and desires to provide for the daily printing and distribution of Tucson Daily Citizen Monday through Saturday commencing with the effective date hereof by TUCSON NEWSPAPERS, INC., hereinafter called "TNI"; and

WHEREAS Arden Publishing Company, hereinafter called "Star," is the publisher of The Arizona Daily Star; and

WHEREAS Citizen and Star intend to publish a joint Sunday newspaper; and

WHEREAS Citizen is the owner of an undivided one-half interest in all of the equipment, machinery, vehicles and other properties necessary to print and distribute the Tucson Daily Citizen and has heretofore placed TNI in possession of said property; and

WHEREAS Citizen desires to employ TNI to print the Tucson Daily Citizen, to sell advertising space for Citizen in combination with the sale of advertising space for Star and/or the joint Sunday newspaper owned by Citizen and Star (hereinafter referred to as the sale of "combination advertising"), and to distribute the Tucson Daily Citizen.

NOW, THEREFORE, for and in consideration of the mutual promises of the parties, it is agreed as follows:

I

TNI is hereby given the right to possession of all Citizen's equipment, machinery and properties necessary to print the Tucson Daily Citizen, to sell combination advertising for Citizen, to distribute the Tucson Daily Citizen, and to operate business and accounting functions for Citizen necessary to the performance of such services. TNI shall determine the gross revenue allocable to Citizen from advertising and circulation sales made on behalf of Citizen as follows:

a. TNI shall determine and allocate to Citizen the gross revenue from national, local display and classified advertising sold on behalf of Citizen.

b. TNI shall determine and allocate to Citizen its gross revenue from the sale and circulation of the Tucson Daily Citizen.

c. The total of subparagraphs a and b, together with any other revenue from any sources derived by TNI on behalf of Citizen shall constitute the total revenue allocable to Citizen by TNI.

TNI after deducting its expenses allocable to Citizen shall pay over to Citizen the net revenue allocable to Citizen and any other revenue from any source derived by TNI on behalf of Citizen.

II

TNI shall perform the following functions on behalf of Citizen:

a. TNI shall act ad combination advertising sales agent for the distribution of the Tucson Daily Citizen. All advertising and subscription rates shall be established by Citizen. TNI shall furnish Citizen such cost and accounting data as may be necessary or appropriate to enable Citizen to establish such rates. TNI shall offer each purchaser of combination advertising a discount rate which reflects the cost savings resulting from the composition of advertising material previously used or to be used by Star and/or the joint Sunday newspaper owned by Citizen and Star. The discount used as the basis for determining the combined advertising rates billed by TNI shall be accumulated by TNI and periodically charged equally against the revenues of the newspapers participating in the combination advertising, that is, Citizen and Star or Citizen and the joint Sunday. The discount rate shall reflect direct and indirect cost savings arising from combination advertising and shall be determined from time to time by a national accounting firm in accordance with generally accepted principles of accounting.

b. Citizen alone shall sell its single paper advertising and shall have the right to obtain orders for combination advertising directly (referring all such orders to TNI for processing) and shall be responsible for the promotion of the advertising and circulation of Citizen. Citizen is entitled to make sales of subscriptions and sell newspapers separately from the carriers under contract to TNI.

c. TNI shall independently determine the expenses to be charged to Citizen in the manner hereinafter set forth in Article IV.

III

Production and Distribution Operations of TNI

TNI shall perform the following operations as printing company for Citizen:

a. Purchase its supplies and all equipment required for replacement and shall print Citizen's newspapers and distribute them.

b. Carry on the general business affairs for the commercial functions of TNI and Citizen.

c. Keep all machinery and equipment in repair.

d. Bill and collect all accounts receivable of Citizen.

IV

Allocation of Production and Distribution Expenses

TNI in its operations shall allocate the production and distribution expenses of all of its operations as follows:

a. Except for the expense items set forth on Exhibit A, TNI shall allocate to Citizen in accordance with generally accepted principles of cost accounting the actual expenses incurred by TNI in acting as advertising sales agent, distribution agent and as printing company for Citizen.

b. TNI shall allocate as additional expense to Citizen the actual cost of newsprint used by Citizen and an amount which will reflect costs in excess of production norms as shall be established from time to time by TNI.

c. In addition to the above set forth specific surcharge items, TNI shall charge the actual costs of any unusual expenses caused by and incurred on behalf of Citizen.

d. TNI shall furnish its accountants with all information necessary to produce where feasible a factor or factors which may be used to reflect the additional costs giving rise to any of the foregoing surcharges and which may be used by TNI in charging said extra expenses to Citizen.

e. TNI shall keep sufficiently detailed records of all of its activities in order that the same may be verified as conforming to the terms and principles of this Agreement by periodic audits by such national certified public accounting firm.

V

Separate Accounting

Inasmuch as TNI will be acting as an independent agent in connection with the performance of printing, distribution and other services for Citizen and Star, TNI shall maintain an independent and separate accounting of its activities on behalf of Citizen.

VI

Termination

This Agreement shall terminate June 1, 1990; provided, however, that this Agreement shall automatically extend for additional periods of twenty-five (25) years unless Citizen gives to TNI written notice of its intention not to renew this Agreement, which written notice shall be given by registered mail not less than two (2) years prior to the termination of the original term of this Agreement or not less than two (2) years prior to the expiration of any renewal period hereof.

VII

Miscellaneous

The parties to this Agreement each agree with the other to take any corporate or other action that may be necessary at any time to carry out and give full force and effect to the provisions of this Agreement, including renewal of its corporate charter as may hereafter become necessary during the term of this Agreement.

The provisions of this Agreement shall be binding upon and inure to the benefit of the parties to this Agreement, their successors and assigns, whether individual or corporate, including, but not limited to, any assigns hereafter created by virtue of any reorganization, merger, or other transactions.

EXHIBIT A

Expenses to be allocated equally between Citizen and Star:

1. Real and personal property taxes and interest on real property assessments.

2. Fire and casualty and all other general insurance.

3. Utilities including water and gas but excepting electrical power (which is primarily attributable to press use and shall be allocated proportionately between users).

JOINT VENTURE AGREEMENT

THIS AGREEMENT by and between ARDEN PUBLISHING COMPANY, a corporation, publisher of The Arizona Daily Star, hereinafter referred to as "Star," and CITIZEN PUBLISHING COMPANY, a corporation, publisher of the Tucson Daily Citizen, hereinafter referred to as "Citizen," and TUCSON NEWSPAPERS, INC., a corporation, hereinafter referred to as "TNI";

WITNESSETH THAT:

I

TNI print and perform all other commercial operations for a Sunday newspaper as a joint venture on behalf of Star and Citizen and shall keep a separate account of all of its activities with respect to the joint Sunday newspaper.

II

TNI shall keep a record of and charge the joint venture with the direct costs incurred by TNI in connection with the joint Sunday paper and in addition shall charge a factor thereof fairly representing direct costs that cannot be separately accounted for and a factor fairly representing indirect expense of operating TNI in connection with the joint Sunday newspaper. The foregoing factors shall be determined by a national accounting firm and filed with the Secretary of TNI.

III

The net revenues from the joint Sunday operation shall be determined by TNI and verified by a national accounting firm and paid in equal shares to Star and Citizen.

IV

Editorial Management of the Sunday Newspaper

A. All live news, sports content and feature sections shall be under the direction of a Sunday editor who shall be appointed jointly by Star and Citizen, which shall provide such staff assistance as they may mutually determine.

B. The comic sections shall consist of all comic sections provided by Star and Citizen.

C. The editorial pages of the joint Sunday newspaper shall be under the direction of the Sunday Editor and Star and Citizen shall have the right to equal space for editorial comment.

V

Each joint venturer shall keep an accurate record of its payroll expense and any other direct expense it incurs in the production of the joint Sunday newspaper. A national accounting firm shall determine factors for Star and Citizen to reflect their respective indirect expense in producing the Sunday newspaper, which factors shall be filed with the Secretary of TNI. The direct and indirect expenses of Citizen shall be reimbursed to Citizen by TNI from the gross Sunday revenues.

VI

All expenses for syndicated columnists, syndicated news magazines, and any other expense customarily incurred in connection with a Sunday issue shall be paid by TNI from Sunday revenues.

VII

This Agreement shall terminate June 1, 1990; provided, however, that this Agreement shall automatically extend for additional periods of twenty-five (25) years unless either Star or Citizen gives to the other written notice of its intention not to renew this Agreement, which written notice shall be given by registered mail not less than two (2) years prior to the termination of the original term of this Agreement or not less than two (2) years prior to the expiration of any renewal period hereof.

VIII

The provisions of this Agreement shall be binding upon and inure to the benefit of the parties to this Agreement, their successors and assigns, whether individual or corporate, including, but not limited to, any assigns hereafter created by virtue of any reorganization, merger, or other transactions. By way of explanation and not by way of limitation, it is agreed that this Agreement shall bind the stockholders of Star and Citizen, any successor organization of those corporations and the stockholders of such successor organization.

References and Bibliography

Abrams v. United States, 250 U.S. 616 (1919).
Achenbach, Joel. (1989, January 29). The bottom line: What happened to Miami's oldest newspaper was a simple matter of profit...and loss. *Tropic*, pp. 11–15, 19.
Altheide, David L. (1976). *Creating reality*. Beverly Hills, CA: Sage Publications.
American Press Association v. United States, 245 Fed. 91 (7th Cir. 1917).
Anchorage dailies to end joint agreement in April (1978, October 7). *Editor & Publisher*, p. 7.
And now, the crybaby billionaire monopoly publishers want more (1988, July 6). The San Francisco *Bay Guardian*, p. 11.
Anderson, Mary A. (1989, October). JOA law may be at a turning point. *presstime*, pp. 6–9.
Antitrust division recommends approval of Las Vegas JOA (1989, December 9). *Editor & Publisher*, p. 19.
Antitrust report issued on Chattanooga papers (1980, July 2). *New York Times*, p. VI:20.
Antitrust unit opposes Chattanooga paper plan (1980, May 20). *New York Times*, p. IV:22.
Application for approval of *Manteca News/Manteca Bulletin* joint newspaper operating arrangement (1988). Docket 44–03–24–9.
Ardoin, Birthney. (1973). A comparison of newspapers under joint printing contracts. *Journalism Quarterly, 50*, 340–347.
Associated Press v. National Labor Relations Board, 301 U.S. 103 (1937).
Associated Press v. United States, 326 U.S. 1 (1945).
Bagdikian, Ben H. (1980). Conglomeration, concentration, and the media. *Journal of Communication, 30*, 59–64.
Bagdikian, Ben H. (1985). The U.S. media: Supermarket or assemblyline? *Journal of Communication, 35*, 97–109.

Bagdikian, Ben H. (1987). *The media monopoly*, (2nd ed.), Boston, MA: Beacon Press.
Bain, Joe S. (1968). *Industrial organization*, (2nd ed.). New York: Wiley.
Balderston, Jim. (1989, May). The CNPA's new bottom line. *San Francisco Focus*.
Barber, Richard J. (1964). Newspaper monopoly in New Orleans: The lesson for antitrust policy. *Louisiana Law Review, 24*, 504–554.
Barnett, Stephen R. (1969). Statement of Stephen R. Barnett. U.S. Congress, House Committee on the Judiciary. Newspaper Preservation Act. Hearings before the Antitrust Subcommittee on H.R. 279 and Related Bills, 91st Congress, 1st Session, pp. 247–267.
Barnett, Stephen R. (1973, January 15). Merger, monopoly, and a free press. *The Nation*, pp. 76+.
Barnett, Stephen R. (1980a, May/June). Monopoly games—where failures win big. *Columbia Journalism Review*, pp. 40–47.
Barnett, Stephen R. (1980b). Newspaper monopoly and the law. *Journal of Communication, 30*, 72–80.
Barnett, Stephen R. (1989, November 6). Preserving newspapers or monopoly? *The Nation*, pp. 513+.
Barwis, Gail Lund. (1980). The Newspaper Preservation Act: A retrospective analysis. *Newspaper Research Journal, 1*, 27–39.
Becker, Glenn. (1970). Failing newspaper or failing journalism: The public versus the publishers. *University of San Francisco Law Review, 4*, 465–491.
Becker, Lee B., Beam, Randy, & Russial, John. (1978). Correlates of daily newspaper performance in New England. *Journalism Quarterly, 55*, 100–108.
Bigman, Stanley K. (1948). Rivals in conformity: A study of two competing dailies. *Journalism Quarterly, 25*, 127–131.
Blankenburg, William B. (1980). Determinants of pricing of advertising in weeklies. *Journalism Quarterly, 57*, 663–666.
Blankenburg, William B. (1982). Newspaper ownership and control of circulation to increase profits. *Journalism Quarterly, 59*, 390–398.
Blankenburg, William B. (1985). Consolidation in two-newspaper firms. *Journalism Quarterly, 62*, 474–481.
Blankenburg, William B. (1989). Newspaper scale and newspaper expenditures. *Newspaper Research Journal, 10*, 97–103.
Blum, Jack A. (1990). Memo to Ed Wendover, Bruce Brugmann, et al., March 26, 1990.
Bork, Robert H. (1978). *The antitrust paradox: A policy at war with itself*. New York: Basic Books.
Borstel, Gerald H. (1956). Ownership, competition and comment in 20 small dailies. *Journalism Quarterly, 33*, 220–222.
Boudin, Michael (1989). Report of the Assistant Attorney General in Charge of the Antitrust Division, Public File 44–03–13 (York, PA, application).
Bowers, Ian. (1969). *An analysis of the influence of the competitive structure upon daily newspapers' advertising rates and lineage*. Master's Thesis, University of Illinois.

Breed, Warren. (1955). Social control in the newsroom. *Social Forces, 33*, 326–335.
Brinkman, Robert J. (1988, February 29). Newspaper Preservation Act: A review and analysis. Unpublished report to the Board of Directors of the National Newspaper Association.
Brown, Karen F. (1989, August). Factors of success for newspapers in intracity competition. Paper presented to the Association for Education in Journalism and Mass Communication conference, Washington, DC.
Brown Shoe Co. v. United States, 370 U.S. 294 (1962).
Brubaker, Randy. (1982). The Newspaper Preservation Act: How it affects diversity in the newspaper industry. *Journal of Communication Inquiry, 7*, 91–104.
Brugmann, Bruce B. (1989, November 13). The crybaby billionaire publishers win (for now)...so we're going to petition Congress for relief. *Association of Alternative Newsweeklies* [press release].
Busterna, John C. (1986, July 17). *Comments of John C. Busterna re Detroit joint operation application: The effect of restrictive trade agreements in the newspaper industry on predatory pricing*. Submitted to the Antitrust Division of the Department of Justice.
Busterna, John C. (1987a). The cross-elasticity of demand for national newspaper advertising. *Journalism Quarterly, 64*, 346–351.
Busterna, John C. (1987b). Improving editorial and economic competition with a modified Newspaper Preservation Act. *Newspaper Research Journal, 8*, 71–83.
Busterna, John C. (1988a). Antitrust in the 1980s: An analysis of 45 newspaper actions. *Newspaper Research Journal, 9*, 25–36.
Busterna, John C. (1988b). Competitive effects of newspaper chain 'deep pockets'. *Newspaper Research Journal, 10*, 61–72.
Busterna, John C. (1988c). Newspaper JOAs and the logic of predation. *Communications and the Law, 10*, 3–17.
Busterna, John C. (1988d). Trends in daily newspaper ownership, *Journalism Quarterly, 65*, 831–838.
Busterna, John C. (1988e) Welfare economics and media performance. *Journal of Media Economics, 1*, 75–88.
Busterna, John C. (1988f). Concentration and the industrial organization model. In Robert G. Picard, James P. Winter, Maxwell E. McCombs, & Stephen Lacy (Eds.), *Press concentration and monopoly: New perspectives on newspaper ownership and operation* (pp. 33–53). Norwood, NJ: Ablex.
Busterna, John C. (1989a). Application of the U.S. antitrust laws to daily newspaper chains. *Journal of Media Law and Practice, 10*, 117–122.
Busterna, John C. (1989b, March). Daily newspaper chains and the antitrust laws. *Journalism Monographs*, No. 110.
Busterna, John C., Hansen, Kathleen A., & Ward, Jean. (1991). Competition, ownership, newsroom and library resources in large newspapers. *Journalism Quarterly, 68*, 729–739.
Can daily newspapers under a JOA each publish a weekly? (1984, September 15). *Editor & Publisher*, p. 10.
Candussi, Doris A., & James P. Winter. (1988). Monopoly and content in

Winnipeg. In Robert G. Picard, James P. Winter, Maxwell E. McCombs, & Stephen Lacy (Eds.), *Press concentration and monopoly: New perspectives on newspaper ownership and operation* (pp. 139–145). Norwood, NJ: Ablex.

Cannon, Lou. (1977). *Reporting: An inside view*. Sacramento, CA: California Journal Press.

Carlson, Anita M. (1982). The Newspaper Preservation Act: The Seattle application. *University of Illinois Law Review*, pp. 669–699.

Carlson, John H. (1971). Newspaper Preservation Act: A critique. *Indiana Law Journal, 46*, 392–412.

Case, Tony. (1992, August 8). Tulsa Tribune to Fold. *Editor & Publisher*, p. 16.

Caves, Richard. (1987). *American industry: Structure, conduct, performance*, (6th ed.). Englewood Cliffs, NJ: Prentice-Hall.

Cellar, Emanuel. (1963). Concentration of ownership and the decline of competition in the news media. *Antitrust Bulletin, 8*, 175.

Chaffee, Steven H. & Wilson, Donna G. (1977). Media rich, media poor: Two studies of diversity in agenda-holding. *Journalism Quarterly, 54*, 446–476.

Charette, Michael F., Brown-John, C. Lloyd, Romanow, Walter I., & Soderlund, Walter C. (1983, June). *Effects of chain acquisition and terminations on advertising rates of Canadian newspapers*. Paper presented to the annual meeting of the Canadian Communication Association, University of British Columbia, Vancouver.

Christensen, Dan, Dewar, Heather, & Ward, Mike. (1988, October 22). Critics question plan to sell or close *News*. Miami *News*, p. 1.

Citizen Publishing Co. v. United States, 394 U.S. 131 (1969).

Civiletti denies request by Chattanooga papers. (1980, May 15). *New York Times*, p. II:14.

Clarke, Peter, & Fredin, Eric. (1978). Newspapers, television and political reasoning. *Public Opinion Quarterly, 42*, 143–160.

Columbus *Dispatch* defends ending of joint arrangement. (1985, November 16). *Editor & Publisher*, p. 41.

Committee for an Independent *Post-Intelligencer* v. Hearst Corporation, 704 F. 2d (9th Cir. 1983), cert. denied 104 S. Ct. 236 (1983).

Committee for an Independent *Post-Intelligencer* v. Smith, 549 F. Supp. 985 (W.D. Wash. 1982).

Compaine, Benjamin M. (1979). *Who owns the media? Concentration of ownership in the mass communications industry*. White Plains, NY: Knowledge Industry Publications.

Compaine, Benjamin M. (1982). Newspapers. In Benjamin Compaine, Christopher Sterling, Thomas Guback, & J. Kendrick Noble, Jr. (Eds.), *Anatomy of the communications industry: Who owns the media?* White Plains, NY: Knowledge Industry Publications.

Compaine, Benjamin M. (1985). The expanding base of media competition. *Journal of Communication, 35*, 81–96.

Congressional Record-Senate, June 29, 1988.

Consoli, John. (1980, March 29). Chattanooga dailies agree to resume joint operation. *Editor & Publisher*, pp. 8–9.

Consoli, John. (1983, July 16). San Francisco dailies move to seal JOA trial records. *Editor & Publisher*, p. 9.
Coulson, David C. (1980). Antitrust law and the media: Making newspapers safe for democracy. *Journalism Quarterly, 57*, 79–85.
Coulson, David C. (1986). A First Amendment perspective on antitrust law and newspaper chain ownership, monopoly. *Newspaper Research Journal, 7*, 35–42.
Coulson, David C. (1988). Antitrust law and newspapers. In Robert G. Picard, James P. Winter, Maxwell E. McCombs, & Stephen Lacy (Eds.), *Press concentration and monopoly: New perspectives on newspaper ownership and operation* (pp. 179–195). Norwood, NJ: Ablex.
Court denies injunction in JOA dispute (1990, February 3). *Editor & Publisher*, p. 42.
The crybabies strike again (1989, January 4). San Francisco *Bay Guardian*, p. 6.
Dimmick, John, & Rothenbuhler, Eric. (1984). The theory of the niche: Quantifying competition among media industries. *Journal of Communication, 34*, 103–119.
Doll, Bill. (1984, May/June). Chronicle fancy dealing in Cleveland. *Columbia Journalism Review*, pp. 5+.
Donohue, Thomas R. & Glasser, Theodore L. (1978). Homogeneity in coverage of Connecticut newspapers. *Journalism Quarterly, 55*, 592–596.
Drew, Dan, & Wilhoit, G. Cleveland. (1976). Newshole allocation policies of American daily newspapers. *Journalism Quarterly, 53*, 434–440+ .
Dunn, S. Watson. (1956). Advertising rate policy: A neglected area of study. *Journalism Quarterly, 33*, 488–492+ .
Editor & Publisher International Yearbook. (1991). New York: Editor & Publisher Company.
Emerson, Thomas I. (1967). *Toward a general theory of the First Amendment.* New York: Vintage Press.
Engwall, Lars. (1981). Newspaper competition: A case for theories of oligopoly. *Scandinavian Economic History Review, 29*, 145–154.
Entman, Robert M. (1985). Newspaper competition and First Amendment ideals: Does monopoly matter? *Journal of Communication, 35*, 147–165.
Epstein, Edward Jay. (1973). *News from nowhere.* New York: Random House.
Expert's testimony supports joint pact. (1982, July 31). *Editor & Publisher.*
Ferguson, James M. (1983). Daily newspaper advertising rates, local media cross-ownership, newspaper chains, and media competition. *Journal of Law and Economics, 28*, 635–654.
Fisher, Christy. (1992, September 28). JOAs face grim future, *Advertising Age*, p. 32.
Fishman, Mark. (1980). *Manufacturing the news.* Austin, TX: University of Texas Press.
Fitzgerald, Mark. (1984, March 17). Obstacles loom in Gluck's path. *Editor & Publisher*, p. 12+.
Fitzgerald, Mark. (1986, September 13). Delay seen in altering of Evansville (Ind.) JOA. *Editor & Publisher*, p. 51.

Fitzgerald, Mark. (1987 March 7). Public hearing could delay Detroit JOA by a year or more. *Editor & Publisher*, p. 15.
Fitzgerald, Mark. (1988, March 5). Distribution battle. *Editor & Publisher*, p. 11.
Fitzgerald, Mark. (1990, June 9). Anti-JOA coalition adds an ally. *Editor & Publisher*.
Fitzgerald, Mark. (1991, February 9). Shreveport JOA to end. *Editor & Publisher*, p. 15.
Fitzgerald, Mark. (1992, October 10). Blame the union, *Editor & Publisher*, p. 13.
Flackett, J. M. (1967). Newspaper mergers: Recent developments in Britain and the United States. *Antitrust Bulletin, 12*, 1033.
Frank, John P. (1986, June 10). Statement of John P. Frank before the Senate Judiciary Committee.
Friedheim, Jerry. (1989, July 20). Statement of Jerry Friedheim before the Subcommittee on Economic and Commercial Law, House Committee on the Judiciary.
Furhoff, Lars. (1973). Some reflections on newspaper concentration. *Scandinavian Economic History Review, 21*, 1–27.
Gans, Herbert J. (1979). *Deciding what's news*. New York: Pantheon Books.
Garneau, George. (1986, August 16). Newspaper JOA in New York City? *Editor & Publisher*, pp. 12+.
Garneau, George. (1988, August 13). Detroit JOA approved. *Editor & Publisher*, pp. 14–15+.
Garneau, George. (1989, August 12). JOA law under scrutiny. *Editor & Publisher*, pp. 26+.
Garneau, George. (1990a, March 3). JOA approved for York, PA, papers. *Editor & Publisher*, pp. 13+.
Garneau, George. (1990b, March 3). Weekly publisher spearheading national fight over JOAs. *Editor & Publisher*, pp. 42–43.
Garneau, George. (1990c, June 16). Knoxville JOA to be dissolved. *Editor & Publisher*, pp. 13+.
Garneau, George. (1992, September 12). Gannett inks $250 million deal in Honolulu, *Editor & Publisher*, p. 31.
Gibboney, Allen. (1971). The Newspaper Preservation Act. *University of Pittsburgh Law Review, 32*, 347–361.
Ginsburg, Douglas H. (1986, July 23). Report of the Antitrust Division, Attorney General of the United States, about the Detroit joint operating agreement application.
Goldsmith, Steven M. (1977). Antitrust—Newspaper Preservation Act—Section 4(b) of the act does not require all newspapers entering into joint operating arrangements to obtain the prior approval of the Attorney General but only those seeking an exemption from the antitrust laws. *George Washington Law Review, 45*, 572–596.
Grotta, Gerald L. (1971). Consolidation of newspapers: What happens to the consumer? *Journalism Quarterly, 48*, 245–250.
Grotta, Gerald L. (1977). Daily newspaper circulation price inelastic for 1970–75. *Journalism Quarterly, 54*, 379–382.

Gustafsson, Karl Erik. (1978). The circulation spiral and the principle of household coverage. *Scandinavian Economic History Review, 28,* 1–14.

Hagner, Paul R. (1983). Newspaper competition: Isolating related market characteristics. *Journalism Quarterly, 60,* 281–287.

Hanscom, Daniel H. (1982, January 14). Recommended decision of Daniel H. Hanscom, Administrative Law Judge. Docket 44–03–24–06 (Seattle Application).

Hearings on H. R. 279. (1969). The Newspaper Preservation Act, Hearings before Antitrust Subcommittee (Subcommittee No. 5) of the Committee on the Judiciary, House of Representatives, 91st Congress, First Session, on H. R. 279 and Related Bills to Exempt from the Antitrust Laws Certain Joint Newspaper Operating Arrangements, September 10, 24, 25, and October 1.

Hearings on H. R. 19123. (1968). The Newspaper Preservation Act, Hearings before Antitrust Subcommittee (Subcommittee No. 5) of the Committee on the Judiciary, House of Representatives, 90th Congress, Second Session, on H. R. 19123 and Related Bills to Exempt from the Antitrust Laws Certain Joint Newspaper Operating Arrangements, September 18, 19, 25, 26, and October 3.

Hearings on S. 1312. (1967). The Failing Newspaper Act, Hearings before the Subcommittee on Antitrust and Monopoly of the Committee on the Judiciary, United States Senate, 90th Congress, First Session, on S. 1312, Parts 1–7, July 12, 13, 14, 18, 19, 25 and 26.

Hearings on S. 1520. (1969). The Newspaper Preservation Act, Hearings before the Subcommittee on Antitrust and Monopoly of the Committee on the Judiciary, United States Senate, 91st Congress, First Session, on S. 1520, June 12, 13 and 20.

Hearings on S. 2314. (1987). Newspaper Preservation Act. Hearings before the Committee on the Judiciary, United States Senate, 99th Congress, Second Session, on S. 2314, June 10, 1986.

Hein, Ed. (1976, November 6). Preservation law fails to help *Anchorage News. Editor & Publisher,* p. 7.

Heins, John. (1984, January 16). Mr. Pulitzer meet Mr. Bick. *Forbes,* p. 50+.

Henkoff, Ronald. (1988, November 21). Publish, then perish. *Fortune.*

Herman, Edward S., & Chomsky, Noam. (1988). *Manufacturing consent: The political economy of the mass media.* New York: Pantheon Books.

Hicks, Ronald G., & Featherson, James S. (1978). Duplication of newspaper content in contrasting ownership situations. *Journalism Quarterly, 55,* 549–553.

Holder, Dennis. (1982, November). Joint operating agreements: If you can't beat 'em, join 'em. *Washington Journalism Review,* pp. 20–24.

Honolulu City Council moves to Settle JOA suit. (1983, April 23). *Editor & Publisher,* p. 86.

Humphrey, Thomas E. (1970–1971). The Newspaper Preservation Act: An ineffective step in the right direction. *Boston College Industrial and Commercial Law Review, 12,* 937–954.

Hung jury: Trial ends in Honolulu joint pact. (1982, August 7). *Editor & Publisher,* p. 14.

Huston, Luther. (1972, January 15). Publishers oppose rules to expose business data. *Editor & Publisher*, pp. 9–10.

Inouye, Daniel. (1970, January 29). Remarks in the Congressional Record.

International Shoe Co. v. FTC, 29 F.2d 518 (1st Cir. 1928), 280 U.S. 291 (1930).

JOA—A 50-year record of newspaper life-saving, (1982, March 13). *Editor and Publisher*, pp. 14–15+.

Johnson, Nicholas, & Hoak, James M., Jr. (1970). Media concentration: Some observations on the United States experience. *Iowa Law Review*, 56, 267–291.

Joint operating agreement may be terminated in Ohio. (1983, June 25). *Editor & Publisher*.

Jones, Alex S. (1989, August 9). Las Vegas papers seek approval for a merger. *New York Times*, p. D18.

Kearl, Bryant. (1958). Effects of newspaper competition on press service resources. *Journalism Quarterly*, 35, 56–64+.

Keep, Paul M. (1982, May). Newspaper Preservation Act update. (Freedom of Information Center Report No. 456). University of Missouri, Columbia.

Kenney, Keith, & Lacy, Stephen. (1987). Economic forces behind newspapers' increasing use of color and graphics. *Newspaper Research Journal*, 8, 33–41.

Kerton, Robert R. (1973). Price effects of market power in the Canadian newspaper industry. *Canadian Journal of Economics*, 6, 602–606.

Kidwell, Roland E., Jr. (1990). Newspaper joint operating agreements: Market power or mirage. Unpublished manuscript. Louisiana State University, Department of Management.

Knox, R. L. (1971). Antitrust exemptions for newspapers: An economic analysis. *Law and Social Order*, p. 3.

Knoxville *Journal* to cease daily publication; Weekly planned, (1991, December 7). *Editor & Publisher*.

Kramer, Staci D. (1987, July 18). Independents cry foul. *Editor & Publisher*, p. 13.

Kwoka, John E. Jr., (1988). Accounting for losses: The great Detroit newspaper war, *Journal of Media Economics*, 1, 41–62.

Lacy, Stephen. (1984). Competition among metropolitan daily, small daily and weekly newspapers. *Journalism Quarterly*, 61, 640–644+.

Lacy, Stephen. (1985). Monopoly metropolitan dailies and inter-city competition. *Journalism Quarterly*, 62, 640–644.

Lacy, Stephen. (1987a). The effects of intracity competition on daily newspaper content. *Journalism Quarterly*, 64, 281–290.

Lacy, Stephen. (1987b). The effects of growth of radio on newspaper competition, 1929–1948. *Journalism Quarterly*, 64, 775–781.

Lacy, Stephen. (1988a). The effect of intermedia competition on daily newspaper content. *Journalism Quarterly*, 65, 95–99.

Lacy, Stephen. (1988b). Competing in the suburbs: A research review of intercity newspaper competition. *Newspaper Research Journal*, 9, 69–78.

Lacy, Stephen. (1988c). Content of joint operation newspapers. In Robert G. Picard, James P. Winter, Maxwell E. McCombs, & Stephen Lacy (Eds.),

Press concentration and monopoly: New perspectives on newspaper ownership and operation (pp. 147–160). Norwood, NJ: Ablex.
Lacy, Stephen. (1990a). Impact of repealing the Newspaper Preservation Act. *Newspaper Research Journal, 11,* 2–11.
Lacy, Stephen. (1990b). Newspaper competition and number of press services carried: a replication. *Journalism Quarterly, 67,* 79–82.
Lacy, Stephen, & Fico, Frederick. (1989, August). *Financial commitment, newspaper quality and circulation: Testing an economic model of direct newspaper competition.* Paper presented to the Association for Education in Journalism and Mass Communication conference, Washington, DC.
Lacy, Stephen, Niebauer, Walter E., Jr., Bernstein, James M., & Lau, Tuen-yu. (1987, August). *The impact of central city market structure on suburban newspaper existence and circulation.* Paper presented to the Association for Education in Journalism and Mass Communication conference, San Antonio, TX.
Lago, Armando M. (1971). The price effects of joint mass communication media ownership. *The Antitrust Bulletin, 16,* 789–813.
Landon, John H. (1971). The relation of market concentration to advertising rates: The newspaper industry. *The Antitrust Bulletin, 16,* 53–100.
Lee, William E. (1979). Antitrust enforcement, freedom of the press, and the 'open market': The Supreme Court on the structure and conduct of mass media. *Vanderbilt Law Review, 32,* 1249–1341.
Leuders, Bill. (1987a, December 11–17). The MNI story: Part I. *Isthmus,* pp. 1+.
Leuders, Bill. (1987b, December 18–24). The MNI story: Part II. *Isthmus,* pp. 1+.
Levin, Morris B. (1989, July 20). Statement of Morris B. Levin before the Subcommittee on Economic and Commercial Law, House Committee on the Judiciary.
Lewenstein, Marion, & Rosse, James N. (1988). Joint operating agreements: Can the First Amendment and profits both survive? *Gannett Center Journal, 2,* 107–118.
Lindly, Will. (1983, July 2). New Sunday *Deseret News* prospers in Salt Lake City. *Editor & Publisher,* p. 16.
Litman, Barry R., & Bridges, Janet. (1986). An economic analysis of daily newspaper performance. *Newspaper Research Journal, 7,* 9–26.
Malone, John R. (1969). *Statement of John R. Malone.* U.S. Congress. House of Representatives. Committee on the Judiciary. Newspaper Preservation Act. Hearings before the Antitrust Subcommittee on H.R. 279 and Related Bills, 91st Congress, 1st Session, pp. 337–344.
Martel, John S., & Haydel, Victor J. III. (1984). Judicial application of the Newspaper Preservation Act: Will congressional intent be relegated to the back pages? *Brigham Young University Law Review,* pp. 123–168.
Mathewson, G. F. (1972). A note on the price effects of market power in the Canadian newspaper industry. *Canadian Journal of Economics, 5,* 298–301.
Matthews, Martha N. (1990, August). JOAs and advertising rates: A comparison with monopoly markets. Paper presented to the Association for

Education in Journalism and Mass Communication conference, Minneapolis, MN.
McCombs, Maxwell E. (1988). Concentration, monopoly, and content. In Robert G. Picard, James P. Winter, Maxwell E. McCombs, & Stephen Lacy (Eds.), *Press concentration and monopoly: New perspectives on newspaper ownership and operation* (pp. 129–137). Norwood, NJ: Ablex.
McIntosh, Toby J. (1977, May/June). Why the government can't stop press mergers. *Columbia Journalism* Review, pp. 48–50.
McLaughlin, Craig. (1989, August 2). Bass's beachhead. San Francisco *Bay Guardian*, pp. 15 +.
McLaughlin, Craig. (1990, January 31). For Ex/Chron, no JOA news is good JOA news. San Francisco *Bay Guardian*, p. 14.
McPhail, Bob. (1988, December 14–20). How the big boys put out a newspaper. *New Times*, pp. 8–15.
Meyers, Janet. (1990, June 4). Foes want JOA law axed. *Advertising Age*, p. 6.
Michigan Citizens for an Independent Press v. Attorney General of the United States, 695 F. Supp. 1216 (D. D.C. 1988).
Michigan Citizens for an Independent Press v. Attorney General of the United States, 868 F. 2d (D. C. Cir. 1989).
Michigan Citizens for an Independent Press v. Thornburgh, 107 L.Ed. 2d 277, 100 S.Ct. 398 (1989).
Mill, John Stuart. (1977). *Essays on politics and society*. In J. M. Robson (Ed.), *Collected works of John Stuart Mill*, (Vol. 18). Toronto: University of Toronto Press.
Milligan, Ron. (1988, July 23). Proposed JOA amendment draws opposition. *Editor & Publisher*, pp. 16–17.
Milton, John. (1951). Areopagitica, 1644. In George H. Sabine (Ed.), *John Milton: Areopagitica and Of Education*. Northbrook, IL: Ahm.
Moore, Donald R. (1979). Recommended decision of Donald R. Moore, Administrative Law Judge, Docket 44–03–24–4 (Cincinnati application).
Mortimer, William James. (1989, January). JOAs: An idea whose time is still with us. *The Quill*, pp. 28–29.
Morton, John. (1981). Testimony before the Attorney General of the United States, Docket 44–03–24–06 (Seattle application, transcript pages 275–277).
Morton, John. (1989, July 20). Statement of John Morton before the Subcommittee on Economic and Commercial Law, House Committee on the Judiciary.
Nafziger, Ralph O., & Barnhart, Thomas F. (1946). Red Wing and its daily newspaper, In *The Community Basis for Postwar Planning*. Minneapolis: University of Minnesota Press.
Naughton, Keith, & Gruley, Bryan. (1989, December 3). JOA startup: Anything that can go wrong does. *Detroit News and Free Press*, p. 1A.
Needelman, Morton (1987, December 29). Recommended decision of Morton Needelman, Administrative Law Judge, Docket 44–03–24–8 (Detroit application).
Newfield, Jack. (1974). Journalism: Old, new and corporate. In Ronald Weber (Ed.), *The Reporter as Artist: A Look at the New Journalism*. New York: Hastings House.
Newspaper Guild v. Levi, 539 F.2d. 755 (D.C. Cir. 1976), cert. denied, 429 U.S. 1092 (1977).

REFERENCES AND BIBLIOGRAPHY 157

Newspaper Guild v. Saxbe, 381 F. Supp. 48 (D.C. Cir. 1974).

Newspaper Preservation Act, Pub. L. 91–353, 84 Stat. 466, 15 U.S.C. sections 1801–1804 (1970).

Niebauer, Walter E., Jr. (1984). Effects of Newspaper Preservation Act on the suburban press. *Newspaper Research Journal, 5,* 41–49.

Niebauer, Walter E., Jr. (1987, August). *Trends in circulation and penetration following failure of metropolitan daily newspapers.* Paper presented to the Association for Education in Journalism and Mass Communication conference, San Antonio, TX.

Nixon, Raymond B. (1945). Concentration and absenteeism in daily newspaper ownership. *Journalism Quarterly, 22,* 97–114.

Nixon, Raymond B. (1954). Trends in daily newspaper ownership since 1945. *Journalism Quarterly, 31,* 3–14.

Nixon, Raymond B. (1968). Trends in U.S. newspaper ownership: Concentration with competition. *Gazette, 14(3),* 181–193.

Nixon, Raymond B., & Jones, Robert L. (1956). The content of non-competitive vs. competitive newspapers. *Journalism Quarterly, 33,* 299–314.

Nixon, Raymond B., & Ward, Jean. (1961). Trends in newspaper ownership and intermedia competition. *Journalism Quarterly, 38,* 3–14.

Omni Outdoor Advertising v. Columbia Outdoor Advertising, 1989–2 Trade Cases 68,872 (4th Cir. 1989).

Opinion and order of the Attorney General in re application of Seattle Times Co. (1982, June 15). Order 979–82.

Owen, Bruce M. (1973). Newspaper and television station joint ownership. *The Antitrust Bulletin, 18,* 787–807.

Owen, Bruce M. (1975). *Economics and freedom of expression: Media structure and the First Amendment.* Cambridge, MA: Ballinger.

Papers' joint operations opposed in Justice Dept. (1980, May 9). *New York Times,* p. IV:24.

Parsons, Marie. (1984, August). Joint newspaper operating agreements. Paper presented to the Association for Education in Journalism and Mass Communication conference, Gainesville, FL.

Pate, William C., & Winterhalter, Alan M. (1970). Monopoly newspapers: Troubles in paradise. *San Diego Law Review, 7,* 268–288.

Patkus, John P. (1984). The Newspaper Preservation Act: Why it fails to preserve newspapers. *Akron Law Review, 17,* 435–452.

Peterson, Barbara K. (1990, August). *The Newspaper Preservation Act today: An ineffective nostrum for a minor malady.* Paper presented to the Association for Education in Journalism and Mass Communication conference, Minneapolis, MN.

Picard, Robert G. (1982). Rate setting and competition in newspaper advertising. *Newspaper Research Journal, 3,* 23–33.

Picard, Robert G. (1985). Pricing behavior in monopoly newspapers: Ad and circulation differences in joint operating and single newspaper monopolies, 1972–1982. *Louisiana State University School of Journalism Research Bulletin.*

Picard, Robert G. (1986a). Statement before the U.S. Senate Judiciary Committee, June 10, 1986, about S. 2314 (To amend the Newspaper Preservation Act).

Picard, Robert G. (1986b). Pricing in competing and monopoly newspapers, 1972–1982. *Louisiana State University School of Journalism Research Bulletin.*

Picard, Robert G. (1987). Evidence of a 'failing newspaper' under the Newspaper Preservation Act. *Newspaper Research Journal, 6,* 73–81.

Picard, Robert G. (1988a). Measures of concentration in the daily newspaper industry. *Journal of Media Economics, 1,* 61–74.

Picard, Robert G. (1988b, September 24). It's time to revise the Newspaper Preservation Act. *Editor & Publisher,* pp. 48+.

Picard, Robert G. (1988c). Points of failure for competing and joint monopoly newspapers. Unpublished manuscript.

Picard, Robert G. (1988d). Pricing behavior of newspapers. In Robert G. Picard, James P. Winter, Maxwell E. McCombs, & Stephen Lacy (Eds.), *Press concentration and monopoly: New perspectives on newspaper ownership and operation* (pp. 55–69). Norwood, NJ: Ablex.

Picard, Robert G. (1989, July 29). Statement before the House Committee on the Judiciary, Subcommittee on Economic and Commercial Law, Oversight Hearing on the Newspaper Preservation Act.

Picard, Robert G., & Fackler, Gary D. (1984, December). Price changes in competing and joint operating newspapers: Advertising and circulation differences, 1972 and 1982. *Louisiana State University School of Journalism Research Bulletin.*

Picard, Robert G., Winter, James P., McCombs, Maxwell E., & Lacy, Stephen (Eds.). (1988). *Press concentration and monopoly: New perspectives on newspaper ownership and operation.* Norwood, NJ: Ablex.

Preservation act ruled [sic] cited. (1974, October 26). *Editor & Publisher,* p. 14.

Price hike in Detroit. (1989, December 16). *Editor & Publisher,* p. 37.

Radolf, Andrew. (1982, September 18). 32 dailies have merged since 1978. *Editor and Publisher,* p. 11.

Radolf, Andrew. (1986a, February 22). Gannett, Scripps restructure Knoxville, El Paso JOAs. *Editor & Publisher,* p. 38.

Radolf, Andrew. (1986b, November 15). Goals of new joint venture questioned. *Editor & Publisher,* p. 21+.

Radolf, Andrew. (1988, October 22). Miami *News* may fold. *Editor & Publisher,* pp. 9–10.

Radolf, Andrew. (1990, January 20). E. W. Scripps seeks to dissolve Knoxville JOA. *Editor & Publisher,* pp. 22, 31.

Rapaport, Richard. (1989, September). Newspaper wars. *San Francisco Focus,* pp. 91–122.

Rarick, Galen & Hartman, Barrie. (1966). The effects of competition on one daily newspaper's content. *Journalism Quarterly, 43,* 459–463.

Redmond, Tim. (1989, January 4). SF: Toward a one-newspaper town? *San Francisco Bay Guardian,* pp. 11–12.

Reilly, Patrick. (1988, February 15). JOA could save Post. *Advertising Age,* p. 3.

Rill, James F. Report of the Assistant Attorney General in Charge of the Antitrust Division, Public File 44–03–14 (Las Vegas application).

Roberts, Keith. (1968). Antitrust problems in the newspaper industry. *Harvard Law Review, 82,* 319–366.

Roberts, Lawrence. (1982, January/February). Saving a newspaper, Seattle style. *Washington Journalism Review*, p. 13.
Robinson, Steven V. (1979). Individual and chain newspaper conduct versus the antitrust laws: What boundaries do the traditional means of checking economic concentration establish for the newspaper industry? *Gonzaga Law Review*, *14*, 819–853.
Roper, James E. (1985, May 11). Justice Department will not oppose consolidation. *Editor & Publisher*, p. 30.
Roper, James E. (1983, October 15). Supreme Court leaves Seattle newspaper JOA intact. *Editor & Publisher*, p. 18.
Roper, James E. (1986, May 10). Bill introduced to broaden scope of permissible JOA activities. *Editor & Publisher*, p. 12.
Roshco, Bernard. (1975). *Newsmaking*. Chicago, IL: University of Chicago Press.
Rosse, James N. (1967). Daily newspapers, monopolistic competition, and economies of scale. *American Economic Review*, *57*, 522–533.
Rosse, James N. (1975). Economic limits of press responsibility. *Studies in Industry Economics*, *56*. Stanford, CA: Stanford University, Department of Economics.
Rosse, James N. (1980). The decline of direct newspaper competition. *Journal of Communication*, *30*, 65–71.
Rosse, James N. (1981). Testimony before the Attorney General of the United States, Docket 44–03–24–06 (Seattle application), pp. 550, 640–641.
Rosse, James N., & Dertouzous, James N. (1979). The evolution of one newspaper cities. In Federal Trade Commission, *Proceedings of the Symposium on Media Concentration* (Vol. 2, pp. 429–471). Washington, DC: Government Printing Office.
Rottenberg, Dan. (1989, January). Survival by failure: The newspaper embalming game. *The Quill*, pp. 27–32.
Ruotolo, A. Carlos. (1988). Monopoly and socialization. In Robert G. Picard, James P. Winter, Maxwell E. McCombs, & Stephen Lacy (Eds.), *Press concentration and monopoly: New perspectives on newspaper ownership and operation* (pp. 117–125). Norwood, NJ: Ablex.
San Francisco dailies to drop bid to keep JOA trial records sealed. (1983, July 23). *Editor & Publisher*, p. 9.
Sanders, Craig. (1988). Aftermath of the death of the St. Louis *Globe-Democrat:* Are failing newspapers still worth preserving? *Saint Louis University Law Journal*, *33*, 1005–1048.
Scardino, Albert. (1988, November 4). Cox to keep link with the Miami *Herald*. *New York Times*, p. D5.
Scherer, F. M. (1980). *Industrial market structure and economic performance* (2nd ed.). Chicago, IL: Rand-McNally.
Schudson, Michael. (1978). *Discovering the news: A social history of American newspapers*. New York: Basic Books.
Schweitzer, John C., & Goldman, Elaine. (1975). Does newspaper competition make a difference to readers? *Journalism Quarterly*, *52*, 706–710.
Scitovsky, Tibor. (1971). *Welfare and competition* (Rev. ed.). Homewood, IL: Richard D. Irwin.

Secrecy on the half shell (1990, January 17). San Francisco *Bay Guardian*.
Sentinel, *Journal* to end agreement in December 1991 (1990, June 9). Knoxville *News-Sentinel*, pp. A1–A2.
Shaffert, Kurt. (1990). Report of the Assistant Attorney General in Charge of the Antitrust Division. (Manteca application).
Sigal, Leon V. (1973). *Reporters and officials: The organization and politics of newsmaking.* Lexington, MA: D. C. Heath.
Simon, Julian L. (1970). *Issues in the economics of advertising.* Urbana: University of Illinois Press.
Simon, Julian L., Primeaux, Walter J., Jr., & Rice, Edward. (1986). The price effects of monopolistic ownership in newspapers. *The Antitrust Bulletin, 31,* 113–131.
Sissors, Jack Z., & Bumba, Lincoln. (1989). *Advertising media planning,* (3rd ed.). Lincolnwood, IL: NTC.
Sobel, Judith, & Emery, Edwin. (1978). U.S. dailies' competition in relation to circulation size: A newspaper data update. *Journalism Quarterly, 55,* 145–149.
St. Louis daily in JOA announces it will shut down (1983, November 12). *Editor & Publisher,* p. 10.
Steel, Robbie. (1989). Joint operating agreements in the newspaper industry: A threat to First Amendment freedoms. *University of Pennsylvania Law Review, 138,* 275–315.
Stein, M. L. (1984, May 5). Seattle: One year later. *Editor & Publisher,* pp. 16+.
Stein, M. L. (1987, March 7). Battling against JOAs. *Editor & Publisher,* p. 11.
Stein, M. L. (1988, May 14). Latest JOA proposal. *Editor & Publisher,* pp. 7+.
Stein, M. L. (1989, August 12). Las Vegas dailies seek joint operating agency. *Editor & Publisher,* p. 23.
Stempel, Guido H., III. (1973, June). Effects on performance of cross-media monopoly. *Journalism Monographs,* No. 29.
Stone, Gerald C., Stone, Donna, & Trotter, Edgar P. (1981). Newspaper quality's relation to circulation. *Newspaper Research Journal, 2,* 16–24.
Strnad, Patricia. (1988, August 15). Detroit JOA signals higher local ad rates. *Advertising Age.*
Strnad, Patricia. (1989, December 18). Detroit rates unveiled. *Advertising Age,* p. 10.
Strnad, Patricia. (1990, February 26). Detroit advertisers flee JOA rates. *Advertising Age,* p. 52.
xxxxxxx
Stroud, D. Michael. (1971). Newspaper regulation and the public interest: The unmasking of a myth. *University of Pittsburgh Law Review, 32,* 595–606.
Takeuchi, Floyd K. (1992, September 3). Gannett purchases Advertiser, *Honolulu Star-Bulletin,* p. 1+.
Tebbel, John. (1970, December 12). Failing newspapers and antitrust laws. *Saturday Review,* p. 58.
Torry, Jack. (1989, October 29). High court pursues paper case. *Toledo Blade,* pp. 1+.

Trim, Katherine, Pizante, Gary, & Yaraskavitch, James . (1983). The effect of monopoly on the news: A before and after study of two Canadian one newspaper towns. *Canadian Journal of Communication, 9*, 33–56.

Tuchman, Gaye. (1978). *Making news: A study in the construction of reality.* New York: Free Press.

2 papers in Chattanooga given partial immunity. (1980, November 7). *New York Times*, p. VI:13.

United States Senate. (1986). *Senate Report 539*, 99th Congress, 2nd session.

United States v. Citizen Publishing Co., 280 F. Supp. 978 (D. Ariz. 1968).

United States v. Citizen Publishing Co., Antitrust Division Case No. 1843, 1970 Trade Cases, p. 88278.

United States v. E. I. duPont de Nemours & Co., 351 U.S. 377 (1956).

United States v. Times Mirror Co., 274 F. Supp. 606 (C. D. Cal. 1967), affirmed 390 U.S. 712 (1968).

United States v. Trans-Missouri Freight Association, 53 Fed. 440 (1892), 166 U.S. 290 (1897).

Vivian, John H. (1982). PMs future in the shakeout and reconfiguration of American newspapers. *Newspaper Research Journal, 3*, 69–79.

Walden, Ruth. (1976, August). *Newspaper failure: An elusive concept.* Paper presented to the Association for Education in Journalism conference, College Park, MD.

Wanta, Wayne, Johnson, Thomas J. & Williams, John. (1990, August). *The effects of competition on the content of the St. Louis Post-Dispatch.* Paper presented to the Association for Education in Journalism and Mass Communication conference, Minneapolis, MN.

Weaver, David, & Mullins, L. E. (1975). Content and format characteristics of competing daily newspapers. *Journalism Quarterly, 52*, 257–264.

What went wrong in Columbus. (1986, January/February). *Scripps Howard News*, pp. 11–13.

White, H. Allen, & Andsager, Julie L. (1990). Winning newspaper Pulitzer Prizes: The (possible) advantage of being a competitive paper, *Journalism Quarterly, 67*, 912–919.

White, Joseph. (1990, January 25). Newspaper monopoly fights to pass go. *Wall Street Journal*, p. B1.

Wick v. Tucson Newspapers, Inc., 598 F. Supp. 1155, (D. Ariz. 1984).

Williamson, Oliver E. (1968). Economics as an antitrust defense: The welfare tradeoffs. *American Economic Review, 58*, 18–36.

Willoughby, Wesley F. (1955). Are two competing dailies necessarily better than one? *Journalism Quarterly, 32*, 197–204.

Wright, Robert L. (1969). How to succeed by failing. *Catholic University Law Review, 19*, 177–189.

Author Index

A
Achenbach, J. 115, *147*
Altheide, D.L. 90, *147*
Anderson, M.A. 118, *147*
Andsager, J.L. 102, *161*
Ardoin, B. 99, *147*

B
Bagdikian, B.H. *147*
Bain, J.S. 83, *148*
Balderston, J. *148*
Barber, R.J. *148*
Barnett, S.R. 14, 39, *148*
Barnhart, T.F. 102, *156*
Barwis, G.L. 39, 99, *148*
Becker, G. 39, *148*
Becker, L.B. *148*
Beam, R. *148*
Bernstein, J.M. 155
Bigman, S.K. 102, *148*
Blankenburg, W.B. 78, 98, *148*
Blum, J.A. 72, *148*
Bork, R.H. *148*
Borstel, G.H. 103, *148*
Boudin, M. 50, 62, *148*
Bowers, I. *148*

Breed, W. 90, *149*
Bridges, J. 100, 107, 108, *155*
Brinkman, R.J. 68, *149*
Brown, K.F. *149*
Brown-John, C.L. *150*
Brubaker, R. *149*
Brugmann, B.B. *149*
Bumba, L. 79, *160*
Busterna, J.C. 59, 71, 78, 84, 108, 111, *149*

C
Candussi, D.A. 105, *149*
Cannon, L. 90, *150*
Carlson, A.M. 39, 47, *150*
Carlson, J.H. 39, 99, *150*
Case, T. 116, *150*
Caves, R. 83, *150*
Cellar, E. *150*
Chaffee, S.H. 98, *150*
Charette, M.F. *150*
Chomsky, N. 90, 91, *153*
Christensen, D. 115, *150*
Clarke, P. 98, *150*
Compaine, B.M. *150*
Consoli, J. 45, *151*
Coulson, D.C. *151*

163

D
Dertouzous, J.N. 111, *159*
Dewar, H. 115, *150*
Dimmick, J. *151*
Doll, B. *151*
Donohue, T.R. *151*
Drew, D. *151*
Dunn, S.W. *151*

E
Emerson, T.I. 89, *151*
Emery, E. *160*
Engwall, L. 52, *151*
Entman, R.M. 107, *151*
Epstein, E.J. 90, *151*

F
Fackler, G.D. 98, *158*
Featherson, J.S. 100, *153*
Ferguson, J.M. 108, *151*
Fico, F. *155*
Fisher, C. 119, *151*
Fishman, M. *151*
Fitzgerald, M. 72, 115, 116, 119, *151*, *152*
Flackett, J.M. *152*
Frank, J.P. 66, *152*
Fredin, E. 98, *150*
Friedheim, J. 71, *152*
Furhoff, L. 52, *152*

G
Gans, H.J. *152*
Garneau, G. 49, 50, 71, 72, 113, 117, *152*
Gibboney, A. 39, *152*
Ginsburg, D.H. 48, *152*
Glasser, T.L. *151*
Goldman, E. 104, *160*
Goldsmith, S.M. 5, *152*
Grotta, G.L. 106, *152*, *153*
Gruley, B. *156*
Gustafsson, K.E. 52, *153*

H
Hagner, P.R. *153*
Hanscom, D.H. 47, *153*
Hartman, B. 104, *159*
Haydel, V.J., III 39, 47, *155*
Hein, E. 44, *153*
Heins, J. *153*
Henkoff, R. 118, *153*

Herman, E.S. 90, 91, *153*
Hicks, R.G. 100, *153*
Hoak, J.M., Jr. *154*
Holder, D. *153*
Humphrey, T.E. *153*
Huston, L. 9, 41, *154*

I
Inouye, D. 52, *154*

J
Johnson, N. *154*
Johnson, T.J. 107, *161*
Jones, A.S. *154*
Jones, R.L. 103, 104, *157*

K
Kearl, B. 100, 104, *154*
Keep, P.M. 9, 41, 42, 44, *154*
Kenney, K. 108, *154*
Kerton, R.R. *154*
Kidwell, R.E., Jr. *154*
Knox, R.L. *154*
Kramer, S.D. *154*
Kwoka, J.E., Jr. 59, *154*

L
Lacy, S. 5, 39, 101, 105, 108, 111, *154*, *155*, *158*
Lago, A.M. 94, 108, *155*
Landon, J.H. 79, 108, *155*
Lau, T. *155*
Lee, W.E. *155*
Leuders, B, 24, *155*
Levin, M.B. 71, *155*
Lewenstein, M. 5, *155*
Lindly, W. *155*
Litman, B.R. 100, 107, 108, *155*

M
Malone, J.R. *155*
Martel, J.S. 39, 47, *155*
Mathewson, G.F. *155*
Matthews, M.N. 95, *156*
McCombs, M.E. 106, 111, *156*, *158*
McIntosh, T.J. *156*
McLaughlin, C. *156*
McPhail, B. 115, *156*
Meyers, J. 73, *156*
Mill, J.S. 89, *156*
Milligan, R. 69, 70, *156*
Milton, J. 88, *156*

Moore, D.R. 45, 58, *156*
Mortimer, W.J. *156*
Morton, J. 52, 71, *156*
Mullins, L.E. 107, 108 *161*

N
Nafziger, R.O. 102, *156*
Naughton, K. *156*
Needelman, M. 48, 49, *157*
Newfield, J. 91, *157*
Niebauer, W.E., Jr. *155*, *157*
Nixon, R.B. 103, 104, *157*

O
Owen, B.M. 94, 108, *157*

P
Parsons, M. *157*
Pate, W.C. *157*
Patkus, J.P. 6, 39, 42, 111, *157*
Peterson, B.K. 118, *157*
Picard, R.G. 50, 52, 66, 71, 98, 111, *158*
Pizante, G. *161*
Primeaux, W.J., Jr. 95, 108, *160*

R
Radolf, A. 6, 112, 115, 117, *158*
Rapaport, R. 113, *158*
Rarick, G, 104, *159*
Redmond, T, 113, *159*
Reilly, P. *159*
Rice, E. 95, 108, *160*
Roberts, K. 39, *159*
Roberts, L. *159*
Robinson, S.V. 39, *159*
Romanow, W.I. *150*
Roper, J.E. 64, 118, *159*
Roshco, B. 90, *159*
Rosse, J.N. 5, 52, 111, *155*, *159*
Rothenbuhler, E. *151*
Rottenberg, D. *159*
Ruotolo, A.C. *159*
Russial, J. *148*

S
Sanders, C. 115, *159*
Scardino, A. 115, *159*

Scherer, F.M. 83, *160*
Schudson, M. 90, *160*
Schweitzer, J.C. 104, *160*
Scitovsky, T. *160*
Shaffert, K. 49, *160*
Sigal, L.V. 90, *160*
Simon, J.L. 95, 108, *160*
Sissors, J.Z. 79, *160*
Sobel, J. *160*
Soderlund, W.C. *150*
Steel, R. 118, *160*
Stein, M.L. 49, 51, 68, *160*
Stempel, G.H., III 98, *160*
Stone, D. *160*
Stone, G.C. *160*
Strnad, P. 97, *160*
Stroud, D.M. *160*

T
Takeuchi, F.K. 113, *161*
Tebbel, J. *161*
Torry, J. *161*
Trim, K. *161*
Trotter, E.P. *160*
Tuchman, G. 90, *161*

V
Vivian, J.H. *161*

W
Walden, R. *161*
Wanta, W. 107, *161*
Ward, J. *157*
Ward, M. 108, 115, *150*
Weaver, D. 107, 108, *161*
White, H.A. 102, *161*
White, J. *161*
Wilhoit, G.C. *151*
Williams, J. 107, *161*
Williamson, O.E. 84, 85n, *161*
Willoughby, W.F. 103, *161*
Wilson, D.G. 98, *150*
Winter, J.P. 105, 111, *149*, *158*
Winterhalter, A.M. *157*
Wright, R.L. 39, *161*

Y
Yaraskavitch, J. *161*

Subject Index

A

Abrams v. U.S., 89
Advantages of NPA, 1, 6, 38–40, 75–76, 121
Advertising prices
  combination purchase, 96–97
  comparison over time, 97
  effects of competition on, 94–99
Aginian, Richard, 65
Albuquerque, NM
  creation of joint operation, 2, 27
  Journal, 2, 27
  Tribune, 2, 27
Allocative efficiency, 83–88
Alternatives to JOAs, 76, 84
American Newspaper Publishers Association (ANPA), 3, 41, 66, 71
American Press Association v. United States, 34
Anchorage, AK, 29, 117
  application for JOA, 44
  creation of joint operations, 3
  Daily News, 44, 53, 55–57, 117
  termination of joint operation, 21–22, 117
  Times, 44, 53, 55–56, 117

Anticompetitive activities of JOAs, 1
Antitrust law
  application to newspapers, 29–30
  Clayton Act, 29, 31, 34
  Sherman Act, 6, 29, 31, 34
Application process, 41–43
Arizona Daily Star, The, see Tucson *Star*
Arizona Evening Star, The, see Tucson *Star*
Associated Press v. National Labor Relations Board, 29
Associated Press v. United States, 30
Association of Alternative Newsweeklies, 70, 72
Atlanta, GA
  Constitution, 4
  Journal, 4
Attorney General, role of, 41–43, 59, 62

B

Barnett, Stephen, 38
Baton Rouge, LA, 100
Birmingham, AL, 28, 119
  creation of joint operation, 2
  News, 113
  Post-Herald, 113, 119

167

168 SUBJECT INDEX

Blum, Jack A., 72
Boarman, William, 71
Bolton, John, 66
Bristol, VA, 29
Brooks, Jack, 71
Brown Shoe Co. v. United States, 34, 78
Brugmann, Bruce, 70–72

C

California Newspaper Publishers Association, 68
Charleston, WV
   creation of joint operation, 2
Chattanooga, TN, 21, 119
   application for JOA, 45
   creation of joint operation, 2–3
   News-Free Press, 45, 53, 55
   termination of joint operation, 21
   Times, 45, 53, 55–57
Cincinnati, OH, 28, 58, 119
   application for JOA, 44–45
   creation of joint operation, 3
   Enquirer, 44, 53, 55
   Post, 13, 44–45, 53, 55–58, 119
Circulation, effects of competition on, 98
Circulation spiral, 48, 81–82, 96
   defined, 52
   examples, of, 56
Citizen Publishing Co. v. United States, 3, 5–6, 25, 27, 29–35, 77
Citizens for an Independent Press, 72, 73
Citizens Independent Newspapers Committee, 72
Civiletti, Benjamin, 45
Clayton Act, *see* Antitrust law
Columbus, OH, 29, 113–114
   Citizen-Journal, 113–114
   Dispatch, 114
   termination of joint operation, 6, 113–114
Committee for an Independent Post-Intelligencer, 53, 58
   v. Hearst Corp. 47
   v. Smith, 47
Communications Workers of America, 71
Competition
   declining, 26–29
   effects on advertising prices, 94–99
   intensity of, 105, 108–109
   measurement of, 108–109
   other publications and JOAs, 3

Congressional hearings, 35–39
Consumer surplus, 85–88
Content in newspapers
   diversity of, 99–102
      arguments against, 89–92
      arguments for, 88–89
   effects of competition, 99–109
   longitudinal studies, 104–107
   measurement of, 91
Controversies re NPA, recent, 2
Cox Enterprises, 2, 4, 22, 115
Cross-elasticity of demand, 78–79

D

DeConcini, Dennis, 66–68
Derrick Publishing, 118
Definitions
   allocative efficiency, 83
   cartel, 25
   equity, 84
   joint monopoly, 4
      in Bristol, VA, 23
      in Madison, WI, 23
      in Lincoln, NE, 23
   joint operating agreements (JOAs), 1, 14
   joint operations, 2
   limited joint operations, 5–6
   printing contracts of weekly newspapers, 4–5
   technical efficiency, 84
Detroit, MI, 2, 4, 28, 60, 71–72, 97
   application for JOA, 48
   creation of joint operation, 3
   Free Press, 48, 54–59, 97
   News, 48, 54–55, 59, 97
Disadvantages of NPA, 6, 36–39, 122
Donrey, 50
Downward spiral, *see* Circulation spiral

E

Economics of newspapers, 4, 76–88; *see also* Structural characteristics of newspapers
Electronic information delivery, 63, 66
El Paso, 11, 27, 112, 119
   creation of joint operation, 2
   Herald-Post, 113, 119
   Times, 112
Emerson, Thomas, 89
Equity, 84–88

Evansville, 27
  creation of joint operation, 2
  Courier, 112
  Press, 112, 118

F

Failing newspaper, 33–35
  factors considered in determining, 45, 47–48
  failing firm defense, 34
  intentional, 2, 57–59
  and predation, 59
  as a qualification for NPA, 122–123, 125
  tests of, 42, 51–57, 61–62
Failing Newspaper Act, 35–36
Financial commitment, 100–101
Financial losses
  examples of, 57
  formulae for covering, 16–19
Fort Wayne, IN, 119
  creation of joint operation, 2
Frank, John, 65
Franklin-Oil City, PA, 22
  News-Herald, 118
  termination of JOA, 118
Freidheim, Jerry, 71

G

Gannett, 11–13, 48, 112, 116
Graphics Communications International Union, 71

H

Hanson, Arthur B., 38
Hatch, Orrin, 63–65, 68–70
Hayden, Carl, 36
Hearst, 11–13, 27
Heflin, Howell, 66
Holmes, Oliver Wendell, 89
Honolulu, HI, 28
  creation of joint operation, 3

I

Information about JOAs
  newspaper attempts to keep from public, 9
  where obtained, 6–9
Inouye, Daniel, 36, 63, 65, 68–70
International Shoe Co. v. FTC, 34

J

Joint venture JOAs, structure of, 9–13
Jones, Richard L., Jr., 27

K

Knight-Kidder, 11–13, 22, 48, 115
Knoxville, 22, 29, 112, 118
  creation of joint operation, 2
  Journal, 112, 117
  Journal Corporation, 117
  News Sentinel, 112, 117
  termination of joint operation, 6, 22, 118

L

Las Vegas, 28
  application for JOA, 50–51
  creation of joint operation, 3
  Review-Journal, 50–51, 54–56
  Sun, 50, 54–57
Legislative history of NPA, 3, 5–6, 25–28, 35–39
Legislation regarding NPA, 2, 3, 63–71
Levin, Morris, B., 71
Limited joint operations, 5–6
  advantages of, 82–83, 122–130
  by amendment to NPA, 130–133
  compared to NPA, 33, 35, 37–40, 75, 87–88, 92, 99, 123–124, 126, 128
  by eliminating NPA, 131–132
  empirical tests of, 94
  in Tucson, 26, 37–40
Lincoln, NE, 6, 11, 23
  creation of joint operation, 2

M

Madison, WI, 6, 11, 23, 27
  creation of joint operation, 2
Management of JOAs
  composition of, 18, 20–21
  decision-making procedures, 18, 20–21
  deliberate failure, 2
  duration of JOAs, 14–16
  effect on failure of existing JOAs, 22–24
  financial losses, formulae for covering, 16–19
  structure, 18–21
Manteca, CA, 55, 60
  application for JOA, 49
  Bulletin, 49, 57
  News, 49, 57

SUBJECT INDEX

Market allocation, 21
Market, definition of, 31, 76–79
Marketplace of ideas, 88–89, 91
Market share disparities, examples of, 53–55
Matsunaga, Spark, 36, 38
McLaren, Richard W., 39
Media News Group, 4
Meese, Edwin, 48, 72
Metzenbaum, Howard, 66–67, 70
Miami, FL, 2, 4, 22, 28, 116, 118
   creation of joint operation, 3
   Herald, 115
   News, 22, 71, 115
   termination of joint operation, 6, 22, 115
Michigan Citizens for an Independent Press, 72
   v. Attorney General, 49
   v. Thornburgh, 49, 60
Mill, John Stuart, 89
Milton, John, 88
Mitchell, John, 41
Mleczko, Louis, 71
Montreal *Gazette*, 106
Morton, John, 71

N

Nashville, TN, 11, 27
   creation of joint operation, 2
National Newspaper Association, 66, 68, 71
Natural monopoly, 80
Needelman, Morton, 48
New Orleans, LA, 100
Newhouse Newspapers, 22, 113–115
Newspaper Association of America (NAA), *see* American Newspaper Publishers Assn.
Newspaper Guild, 41, 71
Newspaper Guild v. Saxbe, 42
Newspaper Guild v. Levi, 5, 42, 46
Newspaper Preservation Act
   suggested amendment, text of, 135–137
   text of, 138–140
Norton, James, 71

O

Objectivity, 90–91
Oil City, PA, *see* Franklin-Oil City, PA
Oil City Derrick, 118

Omni Outdoor Advertising, Inc. v. Columbia Outdoor Advertising, Inc., 78
Operating partner form of JOA, 10
Opponents to NPA, actions of, 70–73
Ownership of JOAs, 7–9
   as a factor in determining financial failure, 13–14

P

Pasadena, CA, *Star-News*, 4
Per se rule, 34
Persis Corporation, 113
Picard, Robert G., 66, 71
Pittsburgh, PA, 28
   creation of joint operation, 2–3
   Post-Gazette, 119
   Press, 119
Predation, 59
Profit maximization, 92
Pulitzer, 114

R

Renewal of JOAs, 14
Revenue division within JOAs, 14, 16–18
Rould, Emil, 37
Rule of reason, 34, 67

S

St. Louis, MO, 4, 107, 114–115
   creation of joint operation, 2
   Globe-Democrat, 22, 107, 114–115
   Post-Dispatch, 107, 114–115
   Sun, 107
   termination of joint operation, 6, 22, 114–115
Salt Lake City, UT, 119
   creation of joint operation, 2
   Deseret News, 119
San Francisco, CA, 4, 28, 96
   Chronicle, 96, 113
   creation of joint operation, 3
   Examiner, 96, 113, 118
San Gabriel *Valley Daily Tribune*, 4
Scripps, E.W., Co., 58, 112, 118–119
Scripps-Howard, 11–13, 27–28, 112–114
Sherman Act, *see* Antitrust law
Shreveport, LA, 29, 100, 116
   creation of joint operation, 2
   Journal, 116
   termination of joint operation, 6, 116
   Times, 116

SUBJECT INDEX   171

Small, William A., Jr., 27, 36–37
Smith, William French, 47
Structural characteristics of newspapers, 80–83; *see also* Economics of newspapers
  causing failure, 111–112
Suburban Newspapers of America, 65, 68
Suburbanization, as a cause of a decline in newspaper competition, 3–4
Swope, Julie, 72
Seattle, WA, 28, 58, 60
  application for JOA, 46
  creation of joint operation, 3
  Post-Intelligencer, 46, 55–57
  Times, 46, 55

T

Technical efficiency, 84–88
Thomson Corporation, 4
Thornburgh, Richard, 49–50
Thurmond, Strom, 65, 67
Total market coverage publications, 64, 66–67, 69, 73
Tucson, AZ, 3, 27, 29–35, 36–39, 64, 119, 127, 129
  Citizen, 5, 27, 29, 31–34, 36–37, 64
  creation of joint operation, 2
  modified joint operation agreement, 37–40, 141–146
  Star, 5, 29, 31–34, 64
Tucson Newspapers, Inc., 32
Tulsa, OK, 116–117
  creation of joint operation, 2
  termination of joint operation, 6, 117
  Tribune, 116–117
  World, 116–117

Types of JOAs
  joint venture, 9–13
  operating partner, 10–13, 22–23

U

United States Department of Justice, 9, 50, 66, 68, 112, 115, 118
  position on NPA, 36, 39, 75
  Tucson antitrust case, 3, 5, 25, 31, 37
United States v. Citizen Publishing, 27, 30–35, 37, 39, 77
United States v. duPont, 78
United States v. Times Mirror, 77
United States v. Trans-Missouri Freight, 34
Utah Press Association, 68

V

Vertical integration, 80–81

W

Weekly newspapers, 4
Wendover, W. Edward, 71–72
Whittier *Daily News*, 4
Wick v. Tucson Newspapers, 64
Winnipeg, 105–106
  Free Press, 105–106
  Tribune, 105–106

Y

York, PA, 28, 72
  application for JOA, 50
  creation of joint operation, 3
  Dispatch, 50, 55
  Record, 50, 55–57